BECOME
SOMETHING

BECOME SOMETHING

How an Enlisted Man
Became a Self-Made Millionaire

JUSTIN C. HOWARD

WIT GROUP | ENGLEWOOD, OH

In the interests of privacy, the names of certain individuals have been changed.

© 2018 Justin C. Howard

All rights reserved. No part of this publication may be reproduced, stored in a retrieval system, or transmitted in any form or by any means electronic, mechanical, photocopying, recording or otherwise, without the prior written permission of the publisher.

Published by
WIT Group
Englewood, OH

Publisher's Cataloging-in-Publication Data
Howard, Justin C.

Become something : how an enlisted man became a self-made millionaire / Justin C. Howard. – Englewood, Ohio : WIT Group, 2018.

p. ; cm.

ISBN13: 978-0-9980208-0-8

1. Howard, Justin C. 2. Millionaires—United States—Biography. 3. Armed Forces—Non-commissioned officers—Biography. 4. Success. I. Title.

HG172.H68 A3 2018
332.6324092—dc23   2017961540

Project coordination by Jenkins Group, Inc.
www.BookPublishing.com

Interior design by Brooke Camfield

Printed in the United States of America
22 21 20 19 18 • 5 4 3 2 1

Dedication

To my parents, who loved us and gave us a great upbringing.
To my wonderful wife, Jenny, who remains the brains behind
the scenes. You are simply an amazing human being and an
outstanding mother. You always have my back,
and you're always there to catch me when I fall.
To my brother, Sean, for always helping to keep me sane.
Last but not least, to my friend Darrell. You have been a
tremendous coach, support system, mentor,
brother, and fantastic friend.
All of you are in this book in more than just stories. You are in
the words I write and in who I am. I love and thank you all.

Contents

INTRODUCTION:
From Chaos to Clarity   ix

ONE:
Early Influences and Ignorant Bravado   1

TWO:
Navy SEALs, Here I (Don't) Come   9

THREE:
Damage Control, Professional and Otherwise   21

FOUR:
Who's in Ship Shape?   33

FIVE:
Boxing, Fear, and Playin' Those Mind Games   41

SIX:
In over My Head   49

SEVEN:
Carpet Cleanin' in California   61

EIGHT:
Finding My Shortcut to Success   67

NINE:
STABILITY, TURMOIL, AND LEARNING TO MANAGE THE BIT   77

TEN:
PERSONAL INTEGRITY, ACCOUNTABILITY, AND GROWING PAINS   87

ELEVEN:
MY NEW SUPERHERO   97

TWELVE:
IT MIGHT BE YOU   105

THIRTEEN:
NO SUCH THING AS A PROBLEM   113

FOURTEEN:
READY TO COMMIT?   121

CONCLUSION:
GET YOURSELF A REASON WHY   129

ABOUT THE AUTHOR   135

INTRODUCTION:

FROM CHAOS TO CLARITY

I'm just a country boy who grew up in a small town in Ohio and ended up making something of himself from nothing. By age thirty-seven, I was a millionaire several times over. Now, four years later, I've written this book to help others realize that they too can become something; they too can make something of themselves, even if they start out pretty messed up, like I did.

Part inspirational memoir and part playbook to creating the success you dream of, *Become Something: How an Enlisted Man Became a Self-Made Millionaire* chronicles my journey from a completely clueless teenager who impulsively enlisted in the navy to the owner of an insurance agency employing 300 people.

This transition wasn't easy. I know firsthand what it's like to fail after making a commitment. I know what it's like to be weak when I could have chosen strength. I know what it's like to be defeated when winning was my goal. I know what it's like to be completely alone when I desperately wanted someone to identify with. I know what it's like to be beaten down, I know what it's like to be counted out, and I know what it's like to be at ground zero.

I don't want to feel any of that again, and I'm pretty sure you don't, either. I assure you: if you feel any of those things, you will welcome the realization that at any moment, no matter your circumstances, you can turn your life around.

Become Something: How an Enlisted Man Became a Self-Made Millionaire also explores how the things that happen to you, whether good or bad, are simply opportunities to learn. You can embrace a whole new destiny at any given moment, and it's as simple as making the decision to do so.

How do I know this?

Because I did it.

Today, I know who I am, what I want, and how to achieve it. Unfortunately, I learned almost everything the hard way. My goal in this book is to help you avoid some of the mistakes I made and to inspire you to do something with your life. When you see how out of control I was, how lacking I was in direction and discipline, and how I finally turned my life around, I think you'll be inspired.

There is tremendous power in our decisions; we just have to know how to tap into the strength we have within us. This book tells a few stories, more or less in chronological order, and offers a few truths that shed light on how I did it.

Life doesn't come with guarantees, but if the lessons I learned hold any merit, you might just find they can help you go from chaos to clarity, too.

ONE

EARLY INFLUENCES AND IGNORANT BRAVADO

> *Often the test of courage is not to die but to live.*
> —VITTORIO ALFIERE

*T*here's no explaining why I went off the deep end as a teenager. I had a fantastic upbringing with two parents who cared deeply about their kids and offered my older brother and me everything they could. Sometimes things just go awry.

We lived in the country, and my father was a funeral director and embalmer who worked all hours of the day and night. As a child, I found him fascinating to watch. When the word came that someone had passed away, he would stop whatever he was doing, put on his nice clothes, and take off.

My dad's commitment to his work was pretty incredible, and he was also a good saver. I picked up on that early because he had a stash of money hidden in his bedroom in an old water pitcher. When I was a kid, I used to sneak into my parents' bedroom to steal money from that pitcher.

I know, not cool. It's shameful to admit I was doing that, but I was just a dumb kid—so dumb I didn't even think to take small amounts. Knowing my father the way I do now, I'm quite certain he knew exactly how much money was in that water pitcher. I recall him asking every so often, "You didn't get into the money in my bedroom, did you?"

After hearing my quick no, he would just go on doing whatever he was doing. The fact that he didn't knock me across the room tells me he and Mom must not have been hurting too much for money, especially since my older brother was also taking money from the jar.

Then and now, my father is a funny, laid-back, quick-witted man. He believes in having fun as much as he believes in hard work and is a terrific guy in every way.

My mother is also a hard worker. Throughout my childhood, if she wasn't at work, she was taking classes to learn new skills. She worked in the delivery room at the hospital most of my teenage years, often third shift, which meant she and my father were masters at time management and prioritizing.

My mom taught me a lot, everything from how to laugh and have fun to the importance of not taking myself too seriously. A lovely lady, she's the anchor of our family and the kind of person who believes everything happens for a reason, something I'll get into later.

EARLY INFLUENCES AND IGNORANT BRAVADO

Both of my parents taught me a lot about love, trust, and how to be a good person. There was never any racist stuff or anything genuinely bad happening at home, so my view of the world and the people in it was always pretty open and accepting.

My brother and I didn't hang out all that much when we were young. He's three years older than me, and he took off for Florida as soon as he graduated from high school. I annoyed him in typical younger brother fashion, but we're very close today. I can talk to this kind and loving human being about absolutely anything, and I feel incredibly fortunate to have him in my life.

Growing up, I spent most of my time with my best friend. Uriah and I were inseparable for years. If I wasn't at his house, he was at my house. In our devious early teens, we liked to talk about running away and starting a gang. As far as I was concerned, this was normal adolescent stuff, but now it seems pretty clear that I was stuck in the stupidity of adolescence, a not-very-bright rebel without a clue.

One night at his house at the start of our freshman year of high school, Uriah told me he was thinking about killing himself so he could sell himself to the devil.

He was starting to be interested in satanic music and had just played me a weird, dark record that I didn't much like, but my girlfriend already had her driver's license and was on her way to pick me up. Maybe this is why I replied, "Man, if you're gonna do that, do it for a ton of money."

That flippant comment doesn't even make sense, much less acknowledge the threat lurking behind the words, but apparently all I heard was the word "sell."

Become Something

Uriah kept talking about Satan and other dark stuff until Stacy showed up, but I wasn't worried. We were going on a long hike the next morning to finalize the details of our latest plot to run away.

I remember telling Uriah and his mother goodbye when Stacy arrived to pick me up in her blue Mercury Tracer. I remember going back to my house and watching a movie with her on the couch with my parents.

In hindsight, I remember that night pretty vividly. For one thing, I wasn't wearing any shoes, because when I leaned in to kiss Stacy goodbye, I recall she made a joke about backing over my bare feet.

The next morning, as I was getting ready to head to Uriah's, the phone rang. At that time, we had phones on the wall instead of in our pockets. I answered and heard, "Justin, this is Vicky, Uriah's mom."

I figured she was calling to tell me Uriah wouldn't be ready in time or something like that, but then she said, "Justin, I hope you're sitting down."

I didn't yet know those words meant you were about to hear something awful.

She said, "Uriah walked out of his bedroom last night and told his stepfather and me he had just taken 119 aspirin and forty Tylenol."

Whoa. That didn't sound too good, but what did it mean?

She continued, "We made him get in the car and rushed him to the hospital, but he went into a seizure."

She was having a hard time speaking. I heard the phone make a loud thud, and then Uriah's stepfather came on the line.

Early Influences and Ignorant Bravado

"Uriah went into a seizure last night, and they couldn't get him out of it. They tried, little brother. They really tried," he said, "but Uriah is gone now."

I felt my heart fall into my stomach. I couldn't breathe, much less talk. Was I even awake? Had Uriah's stepdad just told me my best buddy had killed himself?

He continued, "I'll call you again soon, Justin. You are a big part of Uriah's life, and we want you to participate in the funeral. I'll call you."

I hung up the phone and stood in a daze. After a while, I began to cry. I still choke up today thinking about it. Uriah's death was the most devastating thing that had ever happened to me. I couldn't stop thinking about him telling me he was going to sell himself to the devil, nor could I stop thinking about my response: "Do it for all the money in the world."

What a lousy friend! Why hadn't I realized what he was telling me? Why hadn't I stopped him? All the signs were there. I just hadn't paid attention.

We buried Uriah on September 30, 1991, in Greenville, Ohio. I'll never forget that rainy, cold September day when I served as a pallbearer in my best friend's funeral. It gives me goose bumps to this day to think about it.

Not surprisingly, life got pretty tough for me after Uriah's funeral. I had no interest in school, and I couldn't get over his suicide. I missed so much school that year that I was held back for a second attempt at the ninth grade.

Just as predictably, I also began getting in trouble. I never did anything truly awful, but I was always acting like a class clown, interrupting things one way or another. The last straw for my principal came when some kids broke a door hydraulic by hanging on the door. My name was mentioned, and the principal charged me with being unruly. Even though I wasn't guilty, I ended up in court with my parents.

To this day, I don't know why my dad took the news so well. He was pretty tough with us two boys and could send shock waves up my spine if he was angry. I was completely intimidated at the thought of him hearing this news, but all he said was "Figures" or something like that and never brought it up again.

He did speak up in court, though. After the judge said, "I sentence the parents of Justin Howard to be by his side every day for fourteen days of school," my father said, "With all due respect, your honor, I have a job and will continue to provide for this family."

That was that, and the court papers confirmed that only my mother had to attend school with me. What a persuasive man my father was!

Picture yourself repeating the ninth grade, and then picture yourself with your mother by your side day in and day out for nearly three weeks. Talk about embarrassing! That judge was a smart man. This experience didn't completely straighten me out, but it definitely helped.

My mom was working third shift at the time. She was thoroughly irritated at the thought of attending school with me, in part because she was exhausted, but our relationship was so fantastic that no one knew how angry she was.

On her first day in school, some of my friends started shouting things like, "Hey, Mom!" or "Look, it's Justin's mom!" as we walked down the hall. It could have been worse. The people who didn't know me probably just thought I had a tutor.

Since she'd just finished work, my mom usually ended up falling asleep in class. My friends and I laughed and let her sleep, and so did the teachers.

The best part of the fourteen days came when we decided to go out to lunch one day. Turns out I wasn't allowed to leave school grounds during the punishment, so Mom and I ended up being sent to the principal's office. Naturally, I explained that by now it ought to be obvious where I'd learned my tricks.

At the time, no one was amused but me, but I didn't get into much trouble after that. I'd had an epiphany: I was going to take all the skills I'd acquired in my various jobs detasseling corn, collecting cans, helping at the fair, and working at local fast-food restaurants so I could make a ton of money and get out of town.

As far as I was concerned, success was inevitable, even if it had to wait until I graduated from high school. I'd already internalized the simple but essential concept of "Show up on time, do your best, and the check will be there." I'd also learned that promotions were possible if I did well.

About this time, I started spending my free time with a couple of guys who wanted to start a band. We'd go into someone's garage a few times a week after school, smoke a lot of marijuana, and try to write songs. On weekends, we hung from trees, made bonfires, smoked weed, and drank beer. This was a really cool time in my life. My friends and I were pretty wild, but we minded our own business and didn't get into any trouble.

BECOME SOMETHING

At some point in our junior year, Matt, the guy I became closest to, told me he wanted to join the marines and become a member of the Marine Corps Force Reconnaissance.

I had long hair, smoked weed, and wanted to be Jim Morrison, so I didn't know what in the world he was talking about.

As time went on, Matt began to get more serious about the marines, with posters in his room and a growing interest in guns and knives. I found myself getting interested, too. I wasn't college material, and I had no intention of embalming dead bodies like my father, so joining the military sounded all right. What else was I going to do? Bag burgers the rest of my life?

After doing a little research, I decided this was how I'd escape. Since my father was a former marine and Matt wanted to be a marine, I thought, "Why don't I go my own way and join the Navy SEALs?"

With that notion, a whole new Justin appeared. I loved to wrestle and box and already considered myself pretty tough, but once I started doing my homework on the SEALs, I realized I had to reach a whole new level.

I cut my hair, quit smoking and drinking, and started working out. Whatever it took to qualify for the SEALs, I wanted to be able to do it ten times over!

Before long, I was a lean, mean machine ready to take on the world. I was completely into the idea of joining the armed services and determined to make something of myself, and I was certain the navy was my ticket to greatness.

Of course, I had no idea what I was getting into, and I still don't know why I thought enlisting in the navy would catapult me into the life of my dreams. Simply put, I had no clue.

TWO

NAVY SEALs, HERE I (DON'T) COME

> *Do not fear mistakes. There are none.*
> —MILES DAVIS

I was scheduled to leave for eight weeks of boot camp in October, a few months after I graduated from high school.

I remember hanging out at the house with my family, getting ready to say goodbye, like it was yesterday. After lots of laughter and smiles, we took pictures and hugged and kissed. I remember the white car with the government plate pulling up. I remember the young man in uniform walking up and saying, "I'm here to pick up Mr. Justin Howard." I remember hugging everyone one last time and getting in the car, then turning to look back and wave.

I will never forget my mother's face as we drove off. She looked so sad that I thought, "Oh, no. I hope this wasn't a mistake."

BECOME SOMETHING

For the first time, I started questioning my decision to join the navy. Suddenly, I remembered my dad warning me that I would absolutely hate the navy in his "Damn it, boy; you're an idiot" voice. I suddenly remembered my brother saying it, too, along with a few friends. At the time, I'd just wanted to prove them all wrong, but now I wondered what on earth I'd been thinking. I also wondered why I hadn't had this insight before now.

Ironically, the friend who got me so excited about the military and special ops never actually joined the marines. All I can say is that the people who told me "Hey, Justin, you won't like the navy" knew things about me that I didn't know myself. Like I said, I wasn't a very bright eighteen-year-old. Since it was too late to change my mind, I spent the long drive to the Great Lakes Training Academy in Chicago making conversation.

The two men on the drive bolstered my ignorant bravado by answering all my Navy SEAL questions with a yes. Here's a sampling of the kind of thoughtful questions I asked.

Me: So when you're a SEAL, do people just run to the other side of the street out of fear of you?
Them: Yes.
Me: Do women go crazy over you when you're a SEAL?
Them: Yes.
Me: When I'm a SEAL, will I be able to leap tall buildings in a single bound?
Them: Of course.

Navy SEALs, Here I (Don't) Come

Deep down, I must have known I was full of baloney, because late that evening when we pulled up to a big blue sign that read "United States Navy," I was wide awake, my nerves on full alert.

Sure enough, upon entering the building, the situation became all too real. I can't explain what I thought boot camp would be like, but whatever it was, I was off by a long shot.

People immediately started screaming at me and handing me things, and then a man in uniform walked up and yelled, "I'm Petty Officer Thomas. Do you understand? I said, *Do you understand?*"

"Yes, Petty Officer Thomas!" we all yelled as loudly as we could, mostly in unison. Besides yours truly, five other new recruits were being processed; two were women.

"You will do exactly what I tell you to do from this very second forward. Do you understand?"

"Yes, Petty Officer Thomas!" we all shouted.

Then we began to march. I remember thinking, "Wait a minute. This wasn't on the brochure!"

I vividly remembered the brochure. It showed these dudes in black carrying really cool guns. They had lights on their heads and flippers on their feet and were standing on a beautiful beach.

Hmm. Had I joined the navy just 'cause I wanted to mess with cool guns on a beach?

We marched down a hallway to process some paperwork. A bit farther down the hall, I saw people getting their heads shaved. At that, the magnitude of what I'd done hit me.

In short order, I was buzzed pretty much bald and taken to the berthing, the room where I'd be sleeping for the next three months.

BECOME SOMETHING

The berthing was long and narrow, with double racks on each side, maybe a hundred racks in all. Each bed was called a "coffin rack" because the top of the bunk lifted up and all your belongings went beneath you.

I quickly saw that I was going to learn to live with very few items, because the rack didn't hold much. Not only that but I was about to learn a lot about organization and paying attention to detail, things I'd more or less gotten away with ignoring at home.

The United States Navy teaches you many great things. The problem is if you're like me, you think you already have the answers to everything. Some eighteen-year-olds probably do know a lot, but a few of us definitely attain greater wisdom with age.

As for me, there was a whole lot I didn't know, including what would happen the first night in boot camp. If I'd done my homework properly, I'd have known that people sometimes cry at night, especially in the beginning. Fortunately, I'd read that joining the military is a shock to your system. Otherwise, I'm quite sure I would have been screaming, "Holy Jesus, what have I gotten myself into?" in time with the guys who were crying.

The thing is, when I make a decision, I pretty much become obsessive about it. As you will see, this has been part of my personality my entire life. As I lay in my rack that first night contemplating what I'd done, I decided I didn't like this situation one bit. Right then and there, I stubbornly decided the U.S. Navy wasn't where I wanted to be. Perhaps I was driven by fear, cowardice, or a bad case of the wussy syndrome, but just like when I'd made the decision to join the navy that no one could talk me out of, nobody was changing my mind about wanting out.

Navy SEALs, Here I (Don't) Come

I kept this decision pretty well under wraps in boot camp, but I ended up carrying a bad attitude around with me until the final day of my discharge. Needless to say, this created some problems.

As a child, I'd seldom traveled beyond my home state of Ohio. Throughout my youth, if I was unhappy, somebody or something else was to blame. Trapped at boot camp, immature and inexperienced, I decided I wasn't the problem; the problem was the navy!

After a long spell of lying awake in my bunk feeling sorry for myself, listening to a few guys around me crying, I finally fell asleep, only to wake up to all hell breaking loose.

People in uniform were banging trash cans and hitting our bunks, screaming, "Get up, get up, get up, you sorry sunsabitches!"

"You're in my navy now!" I heard the chief lieutenant yell. "Get your lousy asses up!"

We all scurried to the front of our racks as fast as we could and snapped to attention.

"I am Chief Petty Officer Sumpter, and I'm going to be your worst goddamn nightmare for the next two months. Do you maggots understand?"

"Yes, Chief Petty Officer Sumpter!" we all yelled as loudly as we could.

I looked the guy over, thinking he was just the type you would expect to bang a trash can in your face. Just like in the movies, he was fortyish. The uniform he wore was sharp but messy. His hat was on yet cocked to the side. He looked as though he'd seen a lot of alcohol in his day and possibly a bar fight or two. He seemed almost off his rocker but not quite. He covered it well with his quick wit, sarcasm, and experience. You could tell he was respected yet quite possibly an underachiever.

"You will respect myself and Lieutenant Kofler over here to the highest degree because we have earned the right to stand before you just like you will have the opportunity to do yourselves."

That raspy, garbled mess was also a rational plea. I've always remembered this message because it came through so strong and clear. This dude was rough but kind of cool, and his message got to me: "I have the right to stand before you because I earned it, just like you will have the right to earn it!"

That's a pretty powerful idea when you think about it. It was encouraging and profound, but I didn't take the bait. Like I said, I have this blessing and curse of making a decision and just being as stubborn as all get-out about it. At that moment, my decision was "I don't like this one bit!"

Chief Petty Officer Sumpter went on to explain that for the next several months, we new recruits would do everything in unison, including marching to breakfast, lunch, and dinner without missing a beat. When we were seated, he explained, we couldn't speak to anyone around us. We could put up an index finger for salt and two fingers for pepper, but other than those two hand gestures, we weren't allowed to communicate.

They say you don't know what you've got 'til it's gone, and that, my friend, is a true statement. Even though I fell into the new routine pretty well, I longed for Mom, Dad, my brother, and our dog. Having grown up in the country, I missed being free and doing my own thing, but I must admit I learned a lot in the navy.

Navy SEALs, Here I (Don't) Come

Over time, whether I wanted to or not, I learned how to fold all my clothes in the smallest and smartest methods I'd ever seen, techniques I still use to this day. I learned how to make a bed properly, something I also do to this day. I learned how to bathe and brush my teeth properly, how to sew with a needle and thread, how to use an iron, how to read military time, how to test my body, how to make and follow plans, and how to understand my anger, anxieties, and fears on a deeper level.

The lessons I unwittingly earned in the U.S. Navy are such a core part of my life that I regret not treating my time in the service with the respect it deserved. The fact is I wanted out—and the sooner, the better.

Accordingly, as soon as I realized you had to make a mandatory six-year commitment to be a SEAL, I nixed that idea. Why hadn't someone mentioned this at the recruiting station? Four years was more than enough for me.

For that matter, let me just say that my recruiter painted a vastly different picture of life in the navy than I experienced. I'd spent a lot of time preparing myself physically, but absolutely nothing had prepared me for the mental toughness my enlistment would require. Unfortunately, I hadn't yet developed any of the skills I have today, not even close. It's safe to say I lacked virtually every characteristic you'd want an enlistee to have, including self-awareness.

Case in point, on my second day in boot camp, the higher-ups said they'd been watching us new guys interact. Based on their observations, they were picking a master-at-arms, someone in our group who displayed leadership qualities and who would keep everyone in line when the higher-ups weren't around.

Since I displayed absolutely no leadership qualities whatsoever in the navy, it was eye-opening to see them choose a tall gentleman with a deep voice who stood very straight. For the first time, I began to realize how much people judge what you do and say, including how you carry yourself. This gave me and probably everyone else a lot to think about.

My fellow recruits and I stayed on our best behavior for the first week or two, but eventually our true personalities began to emerge. Our new master-at-arms did his best to keep us in line at night when the petty officers went home, but nighttime is when all the fun began.

One guy in our division made the mistake of keeping a journal during boot camp. After about a month and a half—plenty of time to fill up a journal if you're jotting in it daily—someone got his hands on it and gathered everyone together so he could read it to the group.

The kid who owned the journal fought like mad to get it back and stop what was about to truly wreck his boot camp experience, but the group wanted to hear it. The law of numbers kicked in, and there was no stopping this train wreck once the guy who took the journal started reading it out loud.

"Life at boot camp," he began. "Wow, this isn't what I expected!"

So far so good. We probably all found it refreshing to hear that someone else felt this way, since being in boot camp could make you feel like you were going crazy.

Navy SEALs, Here I (Don't) Come

The journal went on to talk about the food, our group leaders, how the day-to-day was going, and how the kid was adapting to his new life. But then the writing took an unforgettable turn, giving the author's unvarnished opinion of almost everyone in the division.

"This guy Washington's about as ghetto as they come, covered in tattoos and acts like he's about twelve years old."

A loud whoop went up from everyone but Washington when those words were read.

"This other guy Dupree you know is gay; you can just tell by the way he carries himself. He better not be looking at me in the showers."

A glance at Dupree told me just how pissed he was.

"James Jasper, this guy is a complete idiot," the journal went on. "I can't tell if he was dropped as a child or is just mentally retarded, but he has to be the dumbest human being on the planet."

This went on for about twenty minutes. If you can, imagine what the room was like. Even as the comments kept coming and the laughter and finger-pointing kicked in, you knew this kid was in trouble.

The nail in his coffin was the last story, which happened to be about his bunkmate. It wasn't the story so much as the guy it was about. When you piss off your bunkmate, you've really messed up.

The kid basically wrote that his bunkmate had B.O. and that he was sick and tired of always having to carry the guy's weight.

The bunkmate's face turned scarlet as these things were read out loud.

Become Something

You get guys from all walks of life at boot camp. Some of them are nerdy and quiet, and others are straight-up gangster with scars and stories. Some guys had been shot before and had the scars to prove it; they saw no way out of their harsh environments besides joining the military. We had some seriously mean dudes in our division, including a professional bare-knuckle fighter who eventually became my good friend.

After all the laughter and craziness subsided, someone suggesting giving the kid our berth's first blanket party. This is when three or four guys take their empty pillowcases to the shower and fill them with bars of soap. Then four guys take two sheets and throw them across the person, with each guy using his body to strap the person down in his bed. Another person at the head of the bed holds a rag across the guy's mouth so he can't scream or move his head. Then the guys with the pillowcases begin to whip and beat him unmercifully. The sound of it is almost unbearable, but there's nothing you can do. Once thirty guys decide you've earned a blanket party, there's not a lot anyone can do.

I remember hearing the sickening thudding noises over and over again, accompanied by an awful muffled screaming and crying sound. I remember staring at the ceiling while they beat this dude for probably three or four minutes before the master-at-arms made an attempt to stop them. He was unsuccessful at first but then slowly began to convince them the kid had taken enough.

The poor guy whimpered for hours when it was over, but you'd better believe he was a new man from that day forward. He was also completely covered in large welts and bruises for weeks. This went unnoticed by the higher-ups because we were fully dressed every day when they arrived. Not only that but the guys purposely hit him below the neck for this reason. The rest of us were reminded of the blanket party every day in the showers when we saw his body covered in these slowly healing welts and bruises. Bruises get worse before they get better, so he was a mess for a long time.

Boot camp was tough, but regardless of what happened at night, no one dared talk about it to the higher-ups. If you did, it would be even worse for you. I didn't have any significant problems, but plenty of other guys did.

I'll never forget the young guy from Texas who sang country music every day. He was pretty good, and most of the guys were cool with his singing.

One day, after finishing a song, he walked over to the window. Suddenly, he punched it, his fist going straight through the shattered glass. He then started viciously driving his arm in a circle around the shards of broken glass encircling the hole.

This surprising act came out of nowhere, since this guy was pretty quiet when he wasn't singing. It was one of those moments when I wasn't sure I was actually seeing what I was seeing.

Just as we were all grasping the gravity of the situation, the poor guy grabbed a large shard of glass and sliced both of his wrists with all his might. He was kind of far from us as he was doing this, and we all began running toward him. Bleeding profusely and singing a country song, he grabbed his military-issue Bible and laid it on the ground beside him.

We all fought to grab his arms and squeeze them to stop the bleeding while one of the guys ran out of the room and found some higher-ups. They stood him up and carried him out, and that was the last we saw or heard of him. I don't even know whether he survived because no one ever mentioned him again.

As far as I was concerned, this horrific deed was a gruesome validation of all the second-guessing every one of us was doing. Boot camp was so tough that some guys actually saw their decision to join the navy as justification for ending their lives right then and there.

On the last day of boot camp, my family came to watch my graduation into the U.S. Navy. Yes, it was a proud moment for me, but it was also heartbreaking. Deep down, I knew that joining had been a huge mistake, one I'd give anything to take back.

Please don't hold this against me; it's just how I felt. For the next four years, I'd be unable to move ahead with my plans to get a job and make a ton of money. In addition to feeling trapped, I was scared of the unknown, of what lay ahead, and I let that fear take over.

The sinking feeling in my stomach just wouldn't go away, and it didn't help to know that the predicament I was in was all my fault.

THREE

DAMAGE CONTROL, PROFESSIONAL AND OTHERWISE

> *Every man is the architect of his own fortune.*
> —APPIUS CLAUDIUS CAECUS

At the end of boot camp, we all received papers telling us where we'd landed for the next step in our naval education as well as what field we'd be working in.

My walking papers said I'd attend A school in San Francisco, at a place called Treasure Island, where I'd spend the next six months being trained as a damage control specialist. This made sense, since early on, when I'd thought I'd wanted to become a SEAL, I'd picked damage control as my area of expertise.

Damage control specialists keep the ship stable. Their work includes firefighting, fire prevention, and chemical, biological, and radiological warfare defense. They also instruct other personnel and repair equipment and systems as needed.

After spending a few bittersweet days at home worrying about what lay ahead, my mom took me to the airport. It was very cold, and there was a lot of snow on the ground. I'd never flown before, so this was a nerve-wracking experience, especially when I learned the aircraft had to be de-iced prior to our departure.

When boarding time came, I said goodbye to my mom, walked on the plane, and found my seat. As apprehensive as I was about the new adventure awaiting me, I'd be remiss if I didn't say how awesome it feels to travel in uniform. The fact is, the majority of Americans love their military personnel. I have never been treated with such respect as when I put on that uniform. You hear a lot of people say we should appreciate our military men and women, but in my experience, most Americans *do* appreciate us. Everywhere I went, I felt just a little bit taller thanks to how I was treated.

I arrived in California late that night and was sent to a brick building in the middle of nowhere. It was late, but helicopters were flying around. Along with a few other new guys, I was sent to a room with a cot, some lockers, and an ice-cold tile floor. This bare room had a single purpose—to house new guys for one night of sleep.

I was allowed to call home, and I will never forget that call. My father answered, and I could tell by his tone that he was trying to be cheerful.

"Hey, buddy, how are you?" he asked.

"I'm good," I said. "We just got to our location, and . . ."

Damage Control, Professional and Otherwise

I couldn't go on. For the first time, I started cracking. I had fought it pretty well until then, but for some reason it all came out when I heard my dad's voice. I did my best to hide the fact that I was crying because he'd taught me to always keep my chin up, but this was my breaking point.

"I don't know what I was thinking, Dad," I finally confessed.

"Ah, come on now, buddy," he said. "You can do this. It's going to be tough for a while, but you'll get through it."

He did his best to console me, but the reality was I did not want to be in this situation. That said, my dad made me feel better, and I will never forget that call because of it. It was the first time I'd ever broken down to my old man.

We talked for a little while, and then he put my mom on the phone.

"Hey, honey," she said in a super cheery voice. "You hang in there. We're all so proud of you."

I told her thanks and that I loved her, and then I hung up. What else could I do?

The next morning, they put us in a van and we set off for Treasure Island. I have to confess: I was so captivated by the scenery that I remember the drive like it was yesterday. The hills and houses and skyline were mind-blowing to a country kid from Ohio. For the moment, the sheer beauty made me stop wallowing in self-pity.

I knew places like this existed thanks to TV and magazines, but I felt like I was visiting a whole new planet. I just couldn't believe how beautiful everything was. As the driver pointed out Fisherman's Wharf, Alcatraz, and the Golden Gate Bridge, I couldn't contain my excitement. We took a winding road off the bridge, and the driver yelled, "Welcome to Treasure Island!"

Needless to say, San Francisco was the high point of my career in the navy.

I was taken to my room and introduced to Chuck, Jason, and Patterson, my bunkmates for the duration of school. I ate, slept, and worked side by side with these guys for the next six months.

To my relief, I soon discovered A school was more lenient than boot camp. The daily routine of damage control and physical training was kind of like working a regular job, although it was more along the lines of 5:00 to 5:00 than 9:00 to 5:00.

We even had liberty to go into the city in the evenings. I believe the idea was "We'll work them so hard they won't want to go out," but we were eighteen and had the energy of gazelles. We could go for hours, and you'd better believe we did.

I was ecstatic upon receiving my first liberty. I couldn't wait to see what San Fran was all about. My roommates and I decided to take the bus and head out on the town, and we told our driver we wanted two things: alcohol and ladies.

He explained that Chinatown was our best bet, but he wanted to take us to the strip clubs on Lombard Street first. At night, that area lights up into one of the biggest spectacles of debauchery you've ever seen, complete with strip clubs and probably anything else you can think of.

No, my rural Midwestern upbringing had definitely not prepared me for downtown San Francisco.

Eventually, my buddies and I found ourselves at a bar in Chinatown called Buddha's. It was tiny, but the only thing we cared

Damage Control, Professional and Otherwise

about was getting a beer without any hassle. We were dressed as civilians, but everyone seemed to know we were military. Most of the bars didn't even card us, probably out of sympathy. Since we were underage and the consequences would be significant if we got in any trouble, we were pretty careful.

The lady behind the counter called herself Mama San and brought our drinks as fast as we ordered them. We drank beer after beer, having fun and cutting up. Suddenly, she yelled, "It's time for a what da fuk!" in her Chinese accent. She lined up shots and lit them on fire, and when the fire subsided, they were ours to drink.

I liked all my roommates, but Chuck and I really hit it off. We shared the same sense of humor and take on the navy. One time, he told me he'd cut off his pinky if it would get him out. We probably connected because our gripes were so similar.

Chuck had a great personality and was fun to be around, so we became best buddies and went drinking every chance we got. We spent one Saturday in a park in Chinatown drinking beer after beer out of brown paper bags.

After we'd been at A school a couple of weeks, we were drinking at Buddha's one night when two dark-haired girls walked in.

"Hey, what's your name?" I asked the one with jet-black hair, olive skin, and braces on her teeth.

"Mandy," she said with a smile. She looked faintly exotic, and I couldn't take my eyes off her. We shared a few drinks and started talking. Later, as she and her friend were leaving, Mandy wrote her name and number on a pack of matches and gave it to me. I was really excited to get a girl's number so soon after arriving in San Fran.

Become Something

I hoped I'd see Mandy out and about, but after a few days, I called her. Once we started talking, it was as if we'd never left the bar. We set a time to meet at Buddha's that coming weekend, but when it arrived, Chuck and I headed into the first bar we saw. We polished off a few tall beers before I remembered to look at my watch. I was supposed to meet Mandy at 5:00, but when I looked down, it was 5:15.

Chuck and I raced to Buddha's, but it was 5:30 before we arrived.

Mandy was standing at the end of the bar with a really harsh look on her face when we walked in. I shrugged my shoulders to say I was sorry just as a pencil came flying at my face.

Maybe it was because she was so cute, or maybe it was because I was desperate, but I overlooked the fact that a girl I barely knew had chucked a pencil at me just because I was late.

I didn't have the freedom to see Mandy as often as I wanted, so I started sneaking out of the barracks at night to visit her. I literally had to climb down the side of the building to get past the guards, which also meant I had to scramble back up, still half drunk, in time to make it to morning muster. I never got caught, but I was always on the edge of disaster. Also, I was always exhausted, which had an impact on my grades.

Mandy and I developed a pretty good relationship, but soon I noticed that Chuck was acting strange. He seemed down and wasn't his usual funny self.

"Dude," I said one day, "you and I are going out tonight to have some fun. You seem like you need it!"

Damage Control, Professional and Otherwise

That perked him up, and we ended up in a section of Little Italy where I knew I had a chance of running into Mandy. Sure enough, she came in with some friends, and I thought this would be a great way to get Chuck out of his doldrums. It worked for a while, but pretty soon, he was down in the dumps again.

"What's up with you?" I asked. "Mandy's friend Sarah is by herself and looking good. She's waiting for you to talk to her."

All he said was "I'm goin' out to smoke a cigarette."

I followed him outside and into the nearby alley. He was pretty tipsy, but it was obvious something was on his mind. I said, "What's going on, man?"

I wasn't prepared for what came out of his mouth.

He said, "I'm just tired of you thinking you're hot shit because you got a girl here before any of us did."

I was absolutely floored. I didn't consider myself the bragging type. Was I doing it subconsciously or something?

"No, Chuck. You're wrong," I began just as he threw a punch that clipped me in the side of the head.

I took his drinking into consideration, but his aggression was too much for me. I didn't deserve that, so I took him to the ground. I'd been practicing jujitsu for years and was in excellent shape, and the ground was where I felt most comfortable in a fight.

Let me be clear that I had no intention of hurting Chuck. I just wanted him under control. Besides, we were in a dark alley with no one watching, so I had nothing to prove.

I got the mount position on him in relatively short order. Sitting on his chest with my knees in his armpits, I tried to talk to him, but he wouldn't quit struggling to get away.

"Chuck, stop it!" I yelled. "Just stop it!"

Instead of giving up, he pulled my head down and bit me hard on the cheek. I could feel my skin tearing and couldn't get away, so finally I said, "Chuck, stop! You win. I'm done, Chuck. You win!"

He let go, and I got off of him, and when he stood up, he was crying.

"If it wasn't for my fucking dad, I wouldn't be like this!" he yelled. "If it wasn't for that fucking asshole, I wouldn't even be here!"

With that, he grabbed a large rock and threw it straight through the window of a brand-new Mercedes. When the car alarm started going off, we looked at each other and took off.

We raced from the alley back into the bar, me all bloody from Chuck biting me, Chuck red-eyed and obviously fresh from balling his eyes out.

Mandy and her girlfriend gazed at us in amazement.

"Just a little scuffle," I told the girls. "We're okay."

Chuck and I continued to play pool as if nothing had happened, but things were never the same between us after that. Frankly, it sucked, and it still bothers me to this day. I'm not saying Chuck's behavior was entirely my fault, but clearly I said or did something that irritated him. The only lesson I ever gleaned from this was that when life is good, don't get cocky and take people for granted.

Although my relationship with Chuck tanked, Mandy and I continued seeing each other. She was a higher priority to me than A school, so my grades kept dropping. Half the time, I was either exhausted from being with her or too hungover to concentrate.

Damage Control, Professional and Otherwise

All the same, I got to know our two male instructors pretty well. They were rugged old navy guys who had seen their fair share of bar fights and fun.

One day, they told us about a new training simulation we'd be doing. A building was going to be flooded, and our job was to figure out where the water was coming in and to patch the holes as fast as we could. They'd already trained us to fix pipe bursts and holes with anything within reach, including dead bodies, if necessary.

As they were explaining this training exercise and how intimidating it was, I stupidly blurted out, "I ain't scared."

One of the instructors looked at me and repeated my statement, only he turned it into a question.

"You ain't scared?"

"Nope, I'm not scared of *anything*," I said with eighteen-year-old bravado. I thought this was the kind of talk they wanted to hear.

Let me just say I was wrong on so many levels! Alas, this was typical behavior for me, as I still hadn't learned how to properly conduct myself. It really is embarrassing, looking back at how green I was at eighteen, nineteen, and twenty.

The instructor just laughed and began the training simulator that represented a flooding ship.

Today, I'm not ashamed to admit how terrifying it was when the building started filling up with water. The work was cold and difficult, but having a goal helped. Working together, my buddies and I successfully sealed the holes, patched the pipes, and shored up the flooding bulkhead sources, but was I ever glad to get out of there when the simulation ended.

As the end of A school approached, I was embarrassed to learn my grades put me last in my class. I was ready to start taking things more seriously, but of course it was too late. The reality sank in one day when the two petty officers in charge of us told us that our grades determined our place in line for choosing our final destination for our careers in the navy.

My heart sank. There were only so many desirable places to be stationed, and since my grades were lowest in the class, I was going to get stuck with the most undesirable place of all.

To my horror, we were then told that one person in our group wouldn't be going on because his grades were too low; that person would have to repeat A school.

It didn't take long for the giggling and finger-pointing to start. Everyone knew I was always late or just mentally absent and that my grades were at the bottom of the barrel.

As the two petty officers began reading off people's names, the guys who'd done well started picking their destinations. Hawaii and Australia and some other cool-sounding places were chosen first and then areas that were close to home. Meanwhile, the people around me were saying things like, "Sorry, man," and "Hey, San Fran ain't so bad," and "Maybe you'll still get to go home for a few days."

When I heard that, anxiety flooded me anew. Not only was everyone else getting to choose their final station but also they were all going home for a week first. Would I get to go home if I was repeating A school?

Damage Control, Professional and Otherwise

I was dying to go home. Spending time in Frisco with Mandy was fun, but I desperately missed my parents and home.

When the final name was called, I knew I was screwed. Glumly, I watched the rest of the guys high-fiving each other.

"All right, guys," the petty officer said. "This has been a hell of a class. We've had a lot of fun with you, and we wish you nothing but the best in your navy careers."

A few guys turned and gave me that "Sorry, bro" look as we stood to exit the classroom for the last time.

Just then, the more burly petty officer said, "Oh, wait, I forgot one more sitting here." After a pause that seemed to last forever, he said, "Justin Howard, my buddy who's not scared of anything, we almost forgot you."

My heart almost stopped. It had been a while since I'd made that comment. I'd nearly forgotten it, but he clearly hadn't.

"I picked your destination for you," he continued. "You will be assigned to the aircraft carrier *John F. Kennedy* stationed in Jacksonville, Florida, but we thought we'd teach you something about fear first. Did we scare ya?" he asked.

"Oh my god. Holy hell. Yes, you did!" I responded, and the group erupted into applause and laughter.

They'd gotten me good, and you'd better believe they taught me a lesson about fear I've never forgotten. I had no choice but to take a good look at myself and admit I'd been putting on an act. Of course I had fears. Only a fool would deny it. I'd been a fool, but at long last I was starting to see the light.

With my naval career back on track, I explained to Mandy that I was going to be stationed in Florida.

Become Something

To my surprise, she said she wanted to come along, too, and we decided to get an apartment and live together off base.

Being young and naive, we had no idea of the difficulties that would come with living with a guy who was away at sea for three to six months at a time, but we were about to learn.

FOUR

Who's in Ship Shape?

> *A wise man adapts himself to circumstances,*
> *as water shapes itself to the vessel that contains it.*
> —Chinese Proverb

*L*eaving San Francisco made me sad, but it was even tougher leaving Mandy behind. She planned to move in with me as soon as I returned from my first deployment and get a job so she could help out with the bills. Then we'd live happily ever after, except that it didn't quite work out that way.

Increasingly nervous and excited to get to my ship, I said goodbye to my buddies knowing we'd likely never see each other again. It was especially bittersweet parting from Chuck. I still wanted to reconcile and be friends, but he wouldn't have anything to do with it.

Become Something

After my longed-for week at home with my parents, I headed for Jacksonville with all my belongings in a seabag on my back.

When I arrived, I learned that my ship was already out to sea. This meant I'd be flown out on a cargo plane and land on the USS *John F. Kennedy*, also known as "Big John," in the middle of the Mediterranean Ocean.

As if this weren't disconcerting enough, the first thing I noticed about the cargo plane was the absence of windows. The other new guys and I were sharing the rear of the small plane with mailbags and spare airplane parts.

Strapping into five-point harnesses on backward-facing seats and wearing self-inflating life vests and funny-looking helmets with large ear protectors and goggles set my nerves on edge. I really wished I could see out the window and get a sense of what the aircraft carrier looked like as we approached.

I was glad I knew about the large arresting cables on each carrier that snag the tailhooks of the jets and airplanes that land on it. When one of those sturdy cables woven from high-tensile steel wire grabs, you stop fast and hard.

I'd memorized the details, and I kept reminding myself that this system could stop a 54,000-pound aircraft traveling 150 miles per hour in two seconds flat in a 315-foot landing area. Nonetheless, landing on that carrier was the most terrifying experience of my life to date.

I will never forget the moment a giant door opened in the back to reveal the flight deck, the vast ocean, and the blue sky. The scene felt surreal. I couldn't believe my decisions up to this point had

Who's in Ship Shape?

literally landed me here, on an aircraft carrier in the middle of the Mediterranean.

As my companions and I stepped onto the flight deck, the roar of planes was deafening. A young guy wearing a helmet and orange vest over his navy-issued dungarees shouted, "Welcome to hell, boys!"

I can't speak for anyone else, but this definitely wasn't what I wanted to hear. I had boot camp and A school behind me, but as always, I was homesick and scared to death. I had to start over, meeting all new guys, and I'd seen enough by then to know that things didn't always work out very well in that department.

More than anything, I was dreading my upcoming three and a half years mostly spent on board this ship. Yes, I'd get time off, and we'd occasionally head into port at various places around the globe, but we'd be out to sea anywhere from three to six months at a time. I wasn't worried about getting claustrophobic on board the ship, but it did cross my mind that I might get seasick. I had no idea how seaworthy I might be.

If not seasick, I was certainly going to have to learn to cope with the nonstop noise. Aircraft carriers are massive, filled with jets and carts driving all over and hundreds of people yelling and moving. Planes headed out in circular formation for training and came back to land at all hours of the day and night. It was intense and fast-paced, and it never stopped.

The other new guys and I were quickly whisked into the interior of the ship, and right away I realized I'd better pay attention to my surroundings. The narrow passageways seemed to go on forever, and the watertight doorways were relatively small. If I wasn't careful, I was going to be hitting my head a lot.

Two young men gave us a tour, explaining things as we went. We walked past the "chow" area where we'd have breakfast, lunch, and dinner and found the mailroom, the medical room, and a small commissary where we could buy hygiene items and whatnot. Then, based on the jobs we'd been assigned, we met our higher-ups in the appropriate division.

Since I was a DC man, I was taken to the damage control division, where I filled out a bunch of paperwork and got my list of assignments. After that, I was escorted to the berthing area. My bed was the top bunk of a coffin rack just like in boot camp, and I was issued a padlock for my rack.

The young man taking me around told me the DC division was training out in the hanger and would return soon and to go ahead and unload my bag.

This was a nervous moment for me. The berthing was large, with forty or so bunks. These were the guys I'd spend the rest of my naval career with, so I wanted to hit it off right.

Soon, I heard talking and laughter coming down the steps. The guys swarmed in, wearing blue jumpsuits with their last names stenciled on them, and headed straight for their racks.

I was obviously new, but no one paid me any attention. The guys just went to their racks and took out books or headphones or crawled into bed and collapsed.

Finally, a young guy approached me and asked, "You just get here?"

"Yes," I answered.

"Okay, cool. My name's Baranta. I'll show you around a little bit."

Baranta was from Cuba and still had a bit of an accent. He told me the DC division had been up all night doing drills and training, which explained why everyone looked exhausted even though it was only the middle of the morning.

After looking at my paperwork and list of assignments, Baranta took me around to all the damage control stations on the ship. Each was equipped with firefighting gear including oxygen masks, suits, axes, hammers, and even the Jaws of Life. Any tool relevant to firefighting and damage control was kept in these stations.

Baranta went over each of the seventeen stations with me and then took me to the halon stations, where we had access to a type of foam you could spray over the whole flight deck if a fire broke out. This foam was a very important part of the DC division's arsenal since it would kill the fire before any planes or personnel ignited.

I'd seen tons of videos of accidents that had occurred before this system was in place, including the fire that broke out on board the USS *Forrestal* while it was engaged in combat operations in the Gulf of Tonkin during the Vietnam War. An electrical anomaly had caused the discharge of a Zuni rocket on the flight deck and triggered a chain reaction of explosions that killed 134 sailors and injured 161. Future U.S. Senator John McCain and future four-star admiral and U.S. Pacific Fleet Commander Ronald J. Zlatoper were among the survivors of that event.

Become Something

After explaining that part of my daily and nightly routine would be keeping these systems in top condition, Baranta took me back to the berthing to meet the rest of the division.

By now, the majority of guys were up and about. Most seemed exhausted, but a few gave me a nod and a "What's up?" The guy bunking below me was really cool; he gave me tips on where to find everything and explained that we always had to be up to muster in the hangar, which is basically the enclosed center of the ship.

This wasn't a surprise. Navy guys really liked your clothes in tip-top shape, including a nice shine on your boots. As rebellious as I might be in other ways, I always made sure I looked spiffy.

After I was introduced to another young man who had just arrived, one of the larger guys lowered his voice and said to me, "Initiation will be in forward D8 at 6:00."

Initiation? I was already trying to stay close to my bunkmate, thanks to the lessons I'd learned at boot camp, so I turned to him and asked, "What does the initiation in D8 consist of?"

He laughed. "Oh, they just want to rough you new guys up a little, that's all. No big deal."

He didn't seem concerned, so I assumed we were going to have a boxing match or something of that nature.

Later that evening, as we were winding down, I couldn't help but notice how jovial the guys seemed about the upcoming initiation. I had no idea what was going to take place, but I figured this would be a great opportunity to show off some skills that would hopefully impress the other guys and keep them from messing with me.

Who's in Ship Shape?

I was a bit scared, but I have to be honest and admit I'd enjoyed my share of fights before and during A school. Even in high school, I'd never backed down from an honest opportunity to fight. I was pretty confident in my abilities, so while I felt a normal amount of apprehension, I was excited, too.

FIVE

BOXING, FEAR, AND PLAYIN' THOSE MIND GAMES

> *Feel the fear and do it anyway.*
>
> —ANONYMOUS

I've been a boxing fan as long as I can remember. When I was a little boy, I used to love sitting with my father every Friday night to watch two guys bang it out. There was an art to what those gentlemen in the ring were doing, and I loved thinking about what it took to perfect the ultimate offense against someone who wanted to beat your brains in.

I started getting serious about boxing in junior high, when a friend gave me a videotape called the *Ultimate Fighting Challenge*. This no-holds-barred, eight-man elimination contest with $50,000 on the line featured two guys fighting in a cage while observing only two rules: they couldn't bite the other guy or gouge his eyes out.

I was fascinated at the thought of entering a cage to fight another person with only these two rules in place. To me, this was like launching X-15 pilots into the stratosphere without a parachute. Talk about making your sphincter pucker!

I remember being fascinated by the relatively small guy who walked into the cage wearing what looked like a white karate outfit. To my amazement, he avoided every strike his opponent threw at him, then shot in and relentlessly attached himself to his adversary; it was a lot like watching a snake attach itself to a tree.

In short order, one after another, this small guy had his opponents banging their hands on the canvas and screaming in agony while the referee, looking as shocked and puzzled as the spectators, began trying to separate them.

It was absolutely incredible to witness this little guy in all white beating guys much bigger than he was with arm bars and chokes. To this day, it's one of the most spectacular things I've ever witnessed!

At the end of the event, the guy's whole family entered the cage to a great deal of fanfare. The winner was calm and relaxed, not even particularly sweaty, while the audience was as quiet as a freshly plowed field of corn as they awaited the interview that was about to take place. No one wanted to miss what this guy had to say.

Finally, the announcer said, "Wow, Royce! You just won $50,000! What will you do with the money?"

Royce, who was from Portugal, joyfully replied in broken English, "We're going to Disneyland!"

Boxing, Fear, and Playin' Those Mind Games

That reply reveals the character of Royce Gracie. He might not have come from much, but he had tremendous love for his family and for Brazilian jujitsu.

After watching this video at age thirteen, I became obsessed with this martial art that almost no one knew anything about. We didn't yet have the Internet, so I devoured magazines and books and videos, everything I could get my hands on that would teach me how to fight like Royce Gracie.

Later in life, after I was out of the navy, I saw the movie *Choke* that followed Royce Gracie's brother Rickson around during his preparations for something very similar to the *Ultimate Fighting Challenge*. This documentary brought to life the adrenaline, the pain, and the glory and made me feel I was part of the experience. I consider it one of the greatest masterpieces of the human mind and spirit ever made.

Rickson Gracie was interviewed several times, and what he said about fear made a big impression on me.

He was asked, "Rickson, when you go into the ring, are you scared?"

His response was not what I expected from a gladiator of his magnitude. After a brief pause, he said, "Of course I am scared when I enter the ring. All these guys in magazines say they're tough and not afraid of any man, but this is stupid to me. I'm very afraid, but that's what makes me good. I accept fear for how natural and normal it is, and it makes me more sharp and in the moment."

Then he added, "Your fears are there for good reason. They are saying, 'I need you to focus now. I need you to muster all your energy and pay attention.' Rather than trying to suppress fears or act like they're not there, let your fears guide you."

I wasn't smart enough to figure this out when I was in the navy, but eventually I came to see that Rickson was right. Even more, I eventually realized that fear is the one thing that can stop you from achieving your dreams. Accepting this fact can be a serious game changer. If you can control your fear while letting it guide you, you can achieve anything you want.

You know that feeling that develops in your gut when you're in a compromising situation? It's usually one of the first indicators of fear, but if you can direct that energy into your brain, you will be absolutely amazed at what you can achieve. I'm a long way from my naval experience, but I have plenty of fears. Today I'm smart enough to admit them, which allows me to use them to my advantage.

For example, when I first thought about writing a book, fears began to creep in. Did I have enough information? Was I even capable of writing a book? How would people judge me? Would they like what I had to say? Would my book help anyone?

It's amazing how fear can get your attention, but the real magic lies in controlling your fearful thoughts and focusing on the task at hand. Whenever you feel fear creep in, try to make a conscious decision to understand it to its fullest. Once you do, let it guide your response.

In my case, I hired an editor to help me put this book together. I wanted the input of a professional who could help me address the weaknesses in my writing, but beyond that, I decided that whether

Boxing, Fear, and Playin' Those Mind Games

people liked what I had to say or not didn't matter. What was important was that *I* liked what I had to say.

A lot of our fears lie in what other people will think, but please understand that at the core of this worry about what others think is . . . nothing and no one.

That's right. Nothing is there. No one is there.

Don't believe me? Picture yourself walking down a busy street. Now stop and look around. No one's paying any attention to you because the vast majority of people don't care in the least about what you're thinking or doing.

When it comes to the fear of being judged by others, I want to make something clear that my dear friend Troy Miles taught me: no one—I repeat *no one*—should be taking up space in your head unless you want that person to be there, and the same goes for that person's thoughts, dreams, and goals. Troy called it "renting space" and told me, "Be careful who you rent to because the rent's expensive."

Your mind is the one thing you have control over. In fact, your mind is the *only* thing you have control over. Look at it this way: your mind is a penthouse, a gloriously beautiful penthouse in the greatest palace that ever existed. This penthouse has marble floors layered in gold, chandeliers of diamonds and rubies, priceless paintings on the wall, and the most breathtaking views anyone has ever seen.

It's your penthouse, and you get to decide whom and what to let in. It's completely your decision and *only* your decision.

Take pride in this, but also take responsibility. For example, while you're reading this book, your mind will probably start

Become Something

wandering from time to time. Just be warned: you are actually choosing to allow your mind to wander.

That's pretty powerful when you think about it. We allow all the great things that come into our lives because we decide to allow them, but the same can be said for the negatives.

Say a friend wants to tell you how badly her boss treats her at work. Pay attention to how involved you get as you listen. Do you become angry on her behalf? Do you want to call up her boss and let him have it?

If the answer is yes, you're taking on your friend's negativity. In other words, you're allowing her to dump her garbage all over the marble floors of your penthouse.

Say another friend tells you his spouse is a lazy, good-for-nothing slob. Believe it or not, this interaction will make you notice certain things about your own relationship. It often happens in the subconscious, but if you're not paying attention, you can easily begin to see only the bad in your own relationship.

The end result is more garbage on your marble floors.

It's true that a good friend listens and is patient, but a great friend will view such situations from a proactive problem-solving mode instead of just listening or agreeing.

This is why I believe one of the greatest signs of love is getting real with people during trying times and helping them see different perspectives. Sometimes this might mean helping them constructively address an unfair boss or a fear-based living situation. Such an approach helps them yet keeps their garbage from accumulating in your penthouse.

Boxing, Fear, and Playin' Those Mind Games

Like Rickson Gracie, you control your thoughts and decisions by controlling your mind. When you feel afraid, dig in until you understand your fear. Use the energy created by this fear to help you make decisions. If you need to face something head-on, look at it as though you're straightening a crooked painting on the gold-leaf wall of your penthouse. If something stings or is tough to swallow, look at it as though it's a leak in your state-of-the-art roof. If you can, patch the leak. If you have to, get a brand new roof.

Above all, take care of your penthouse. Fix what needs to be fixed, but protect your penthouse.

No approach is perfect, but if you can harness the power of your mind instead of playing mind games with yourself, you'll have all the tools you need to go after what you want in life. You'll also have all the tools you need to succeed, which is really nothing more than making the decision to do so.

Since 2005, I've coached many hundreds of people to become insurance agents. Time and again, they have a hard time understanding that regardless of what emotion they feel—anger, anxiety, pleasure, etc.—they're making the decision to feel this way.

This used to be hard for me to understand, but today I embrace this reality. I like to think I'm decent at choosing to live consciously and fully, but I'm nowhere close to great.

The fact that I've decided to live this way doesn't mean you have to, but if you're reading this book, you're obviously searching for answers and making a decision to improve your life. Realizing that you have complete control over all that comes in as well as complete control over everything that goes out is where the journey to become something really begins.

Become Something

Today, after a lot of deep and honest reflection, I understand myself on a higher level than I used to. This allows me to use all my emotions, from excitement to negativity to fear, as pure energy to help me in whatever situation I happen to be in.

I just wasn't yet at this point during my time on board the *John F. Kennedy*.

SIX

IN OVER MY HEAD

> *The more I learn, the more I realize how much I don't know.*
>
> —ALBERT EINSTEIN

I've already confessed that I loved to watch boxing as a kid. What I haven't fully revealed is that when I was in my teens, I decided it was time for me to get serious about learning to box.

There wasn't much opportunity in the farm area I grew up in, but eventually I found a gym in Dayton about an hour away. Sometimes my dad drove me there, and when I turned sixteen, I started driving myself.

I gave it my all, but let me tell you, the kids I boxed were being groomed for greatness. They were *fast*. I went in every week, took my usual beating, and headed home frustrated that I wasn't as fast as they were.

Become Something

I gave up boxing after about a year, but my love for the sport never changed. In my subsequent scraps in high school and beyond, I found myself utilizing the moves I'd learned at the gym and from watching various videos. I might not have been able to compete against the boys from Dayton, but I could usually hold my own elsewhere, and that was as true at my initiation on board the *John F. Kennedy* as it was anywhere else.

Some of the new guys wanted no part of the initiation, but two other fellows and I showed up as scheduled in a large, empty room at 6:00 sharp. A glance told me it was seven burly guys against three pretty scrawny ones, including yours truly.

As we walked in, the seven guys laughed, then pretty much ran and tackled us.

The first guy who came at me was my bunkmate Sid. I put him in a guillotine choke, something I'd first learned watching videos on jujitsu. I basically wrapped my arm over his head and then under his neck. I was really just trying to hold him and keep him under control. A benefit of this position is that the guy you're holding is on top, but to anyone watching, it looks like he's the one who has things under control.

Because Sid was swinging at my face, I knew he wasn't playing. He wanted to hurt me, so I tightened the choke enough to get his attention. He quit swinging at me, and when I released the choke, he was sitting on my chest looking down at me with an expression that went something like, "You little jerk!" He rolled off me and lay there, clearly thinking, "What just happened?"

As I sat up, I could see two on one directly in front of me. They were really letting the new kid have it, so I jumped on the back of the guy on top and put him in what's called a rear naked choke. If done correctly, this move allows you to use the person you're choking as a shield from others trying to kick and hit you.

I ended up putting this guy out cold, and when I stood up, a young lanky dude approached, ready to box. You could tell he'd seen what I'd done to the last guy and wanted to stay on his feet. He kept his distance, jumping up and down on the balls of his feet, saying, "Come on, come on, you ain't gonna be chokin' my ass like that!"

"All right! That's enough!" one of the petty officers suddenly yelled. "These boys have had enough!" The words echoed off the steal beams all around us in that great big room.

The guy who was squaring up with me said, "This ain't over, dude."

This comment made me wonder whether I'd made an enemy on my new floating home, but after chow that night, lying in my rack reading, I was pleased to overhear some guys explaining that once I got ahold of you, the next thing you knew, you were going to sleep. I heard respect in their voices, and that was always a good sign.

I ended up getting along all right, but I was pretty lonesome at first. My negative attitude about being stuck in the navy boiled away inside me and kept me from recognizing some of the good things that were happening, including the fact that I was a pretty good DC man and was becoming friends with Sid. We had similar personalities, and he really respected the skills I showed when we fought that first night.

I even became friends with the guy I thought might become my enemy. He ignored me for a while, but once we were forced to interact, we began cutting up like nothing had happened. At that, I began to relax and find my footing, but I held on for dear life to the fact that my first deployment lasted only three months. As soon as I got back to port, Mandy was moving in. I missed her desperately.

When the three months were up and we were back in port, I asked Sid and a couple of other guys to help me find furniture for my newly rented apartment. We weren't looking for the kind you go to the store and buy; we were "scrapping," looking for furniture other sailors throw in the trash because of a deployment, a breakup, getting out of the service, or some other reason.

One of the guys had a pickup truck, and we drove up and down the streets, the guys yelling every time they saw something promising.

"Cabinet!" one would yell or "Couch!" and the driver would circle back to see what jewel had been found. I talked about Mandy a lot, so the guys were really into helping me. They stuck with me until the bed of the truck was full just so I could have a furnished apartment when my girl arrived.

After filling the apartment, we realized the only thing missing was a bed. The ones we had seen were definitely not usable, so I did the next best thing—I went to the store and bought an air mattress. I blew up my new bed in my first apartment and went back to live on the ship until Mandy arrived.

Once she was in town, I stayed with her as much as possible. Pretty much all we did was drink, but we had a great time.

Sid eventually got a place of his own in a mobile home park, and we spent a lot of time over there, too.

I was now nineteen and Mandy was eighteen, and one day we decided to get married. For one thing, we wanted to make more money, and enlisted guys who were married were paid more. Most weeks, I had to trade the title of my car for a cash loan in order to make ends meet. When I returned the money, I got the title back. Mandy and I were literally living from paycheck to paycheck, so the thought of more money was appealing.

We also wanted to get married in order to alleviate Mandy's insecurity. I was going to be away at sea a lot, and she would be lonely, with her friends and family all back in California.

Breaking the news to Mandy's parents that we were getting married didn't go well. I can still hear her mom yelling at her in Italian over the phone, but finally she agreed to send Mandy her grandmother's wedding dress.

I didn't say a word about getting married to my family. Mandy and I wanted to elope, so why not tell them after the fact?

The day before I was set to deploy for three months, while Mandy and I were driving to the courthouse to tie the knot, I was pulled over for running a red light.

The officer asked for my license and registration and for Mandy's identification and then went back to his car for what seemed like an eternity. When he finally came back, he gave me a warning instead of a ticket and told us to enjoy the rest of our day, but it was a bit too late for that. It was now 4:55, and the courthouse closed at 5:00. I drove like a maniac, but the doors were locked when we arrived.

Mandy was devastated, and I wasn't too happy either. We went back to the apartment and drowned our sorrows in alcohol.

The next morning, exhausted and hungover, I deployed as scheduled, but leaving Mandy crying on the pier was extremely difficult. I knew she was going to have a tough time while I was gone. I hoped she'd be able to find a job she enjoyed, both to fill in the time and to help pay our bills.

Over the next three months, we sent each other lots of letters, and I called every chance I got. Mandy used to spray her letters with perfume and put lipstick kisses on the inside of the cards. When you're out to sea for long periods of time, it's pretty nice to receive things like that, but all those months away gave me a lot of time to think, and something was bugging me about our trip to the courthouse.

It might sound a little crazy, but I couldn't help but think that being pulled over and kept on the side of the road for so long on our way to the courthouse was a sign. I loved Mandy, but I was beginning to second-guess our decision to get married. I was afraid we were too young to make such a momentous decision, and I decided to tell her that when I returned to port.

After three months at sea, Mandy was waving on the pier when we pulled in, a big smile on her face. I was relieved to see her safe and sound, but that didn't mean our finances had improved any. She'd gotten a job while I was gone but had quickly been fired. She explained that she'd been so lonely and homesick that she could hardly function, so her boss had let her go because of her poor performance.

I felt horrible. I tried to explain how I felt about getting married so young, and I also explained that being alone while I was at sea for such long periods wasn't fair to her. Then I asked how she felt about returning to California during the times I was away.

She seemed to take it well, but late that evening, with tears coming down her face, she took a pair of scissors and began hacking her grandmother's wedding dress into pieces.

I couldn't believe my eyes. We were both kind of drunk, but after I got her to calm down and explain why she would do such a thing, she said, "You just don't want to marry me."

I denied this and did my best to explain my complicated feelings, and eventually Mandy agreed it would be best if she returned to California during my deployments.

We kept up a long-distance relationship with letters and phone calls for much of the next year, but then Mandy returned to Florida because we missed each other so much. We immediately picked up where we'd left off, having fun when I was in town and singing the blues when I left.

As always, our excessive partying led me to make some really bad decisions. When I was home, I was either hungover or exhausted from staying up so late. I quickly established a pattern of being late to training or missing it altogether, which meant I was constantly in trouble.

By the time my next deployment was on the horizon, Mandy and I were so tight on funds that I realized I was going to miss the rent payment for the second month in a row. This meant I was going to be evicted, or rather that Mandy was. I would be gone anyway.

Become Something

As the date for my departure drew closer, I impulsively decided to skip the ship's movement and drive Mandy back to California. As crazy as it sounds, I didn't spend any time weighing the consequences. Like I said, I wasn't a very bright kid.

When the day to depart arrived, I took some trash off the ship to put in the dumpsters. Then, instead of returning to the ship, I walked to my car and drove to our apartment. The ship was leaving in an hour, but I'd already told Mandy my plan, and she hadn't argued.

We loaded up my hatchback with as much stuff as we could fit and hit the road. Our destination was L.A., where Mandy's dad worked as a radio personality at an Italian radio station. I had at least thirty days before I'd be considered AWOL, and we hoped he'd give me a job for a few weeks. I wasn't sure what would happen upon my return to my ship, but I was willing to take my chances and hope for the best. I just couldn't abandon Mandy with no money, no apartment, and no way to get home.

We drove all the way across the country in a day and a half. Mandy's dad was supposedly ready to welcome us, but once we arrived, he was less than friendly. In retrospect, I completely understand why he didn't like the situation his daughter was in.

After a few days in L.A., we decided to head to San Francisco so I could leave Mandy at her mother's and return to the ship within the thirty-day time frame.

After exchanging tearful goodbyes in San Francisco, I hit the road for a lonely and nerve-racking drive back to Florida. I'd heard horror stories of people going to the brig for missing a ship's movement, so I went directly to the base to face the music.

In over My Head

My reception was chilly. The *John F. Kennedy* was somewhere in the Persian Gulf, and though a hurricane was swirling about, I learned I would be immediately flown out to join it.

Hurricanes happen all the time in the middle of the ocean, but this one was a doozy. As we approached the ship, the storm intensified. The closer the pilot came to landing, the more obvious it became that he wasn't going to be successful. We were about a hundred feet from the flight deck when he jerked the yoke to pull us out.

He must have realized he'd come in too fast before, because this time he circled so slowly it seemed we might fall out of the sky. We bounced and bobbed through the air until he finally forced the plane onto the flight deck with a thunderous crashing sound. As nervous as I was about seeing my lieutenant and the ship's captain, I felt lucky to be alive.

As my friends caught sight of me walking the halls to the DC division with the flight deck crew flanking me, their mouths dropped open. A few said things like "Ah, shit, man, you're in for it," which did little to alleviate my apprehension.

When I arrived at the division, the lieutenant was waiting for me. He was a tall, skinny gentleman in his fifties, but he looked older, thanks to the stresses of military life.

The two of us had a love/hate relationship. He loved me when I showed up because I worked hard, but mostly he hated me because he had to chew me out on a regular basis for acting like a fool every chance I got.

We were occasionally allowed off the ship while on deployment, and my buddies and I always jumped at the chance to go barhopping.

Become Something

We also occasionally engaged in a good old-fashioned bar fight to support the navy tradition. By the time I was hauled in front of the captain for getting drunk and acting like an idiot at our entry into Portsmouth, England, I'd created a name for myself with my senior petty officers and lieutenant. Needless to say, it wasn't a good one.

Now, the lieutenant looked very serious and intimidating, and he talked to me like a stern father.

"What in the world were you thinking?" he asked. Before I could answer, he continued, "You're destroying your military career, and you're doing it for a piece of ass!"

He explained that I'd be going in front of the captain for the second time, and I'd better have a good reason for missing the ship's movement.

I planned to tell the captain the truth. I'd missed the ship's movement in order to take my girlfriend home to California. We were going to lose our apartment, the ship was leaving, and she had no money and no one to help her. I'd felt I had no choice.

The next morning, I stood at attention to wait my turn. When it was time to walk up to the captain, the look on his face told me he remembered me.

"You don't really like my navy, do you, Justin?" he said by way of greeting.

"All due respect, Sir, no sir," I said with confidence. I was an idiot, but at least I told the truth.

He responded, "I can understand that, Justin. It's definitely not for everybody."

I'd been in for more than two years, so maybe the captain was empathetic because of that, or maybe he just decided I wasn't worth the trouble I caused. Whatever the reason, to my great surprise, he gave me ninety days restricted to the ship. After that, I was to be discharged with an OTH, which stands for Other Than Honorable. This is somewhat embarrassing to me today, but at the time, I was elated.

When my ninety days were up, I said farewell to my shipmates, packed my meager belongings into my car, and headed west. Not only did I consider San Francisco the greatest place on earth, but also I was about to be reunited with Mandy. All I had to do now was find a job, and at long last we'd live happily ever after.

SEVEN

CARPET CLEANIN' IN CALIFORNIA

> *Stay hungry. Stay foolish.*
>
> —STEVE JOBS

I arrived in San Francisco driving on fumes, with no job and nowhere to live.

Mandy's mom liked me okay, but it was out of the question for me to move in with them, so the first thing I did was grab a phone book and go through the yellow pages, calling every company that looked promising to see whether anyone was hiring.

When I dialed up a carpet-cleaning company called Chem-Dry, the guy on the other end invited me in for an interview.

I cobbled together the best clothes I could find and went in the next morning. I must have said something right, because I got the job. Better yet, I was to start immediately.

Become Something

I know it sounds confident, but I quickly stood out from all the other employees. Determined to improve my situation in life, I showed up on time every day and studied the equipment until I knew every inch of it inside and out. I then started coming in early just to clean the machinery. Because the company had a good reputation and the carpets dried fast, I sometimes found myself in the homes of the rich and famous, or at least those who lived near them.

One day, I cleaned the carpets of Robin Williams's neighbor in a beautiful area overlooking the Golden Gate Bridge. As I was leaving, a gentleman across the street was getting his newspaper. I couldn't resist asking him, "Do you get to see Robin Williams much?"

The man looked at me in a half-pitying, half-amused sort of way and said, "He puts his pants on one leg at a time like the rest of us, son."

As always, I had a lot to learn, but I perked up when we cleaned the carpets of a gentleman who told me he was making 14K a month. The year was 1998, and this sounded like an unbelievable amount of money. This same guy drove a brand-new Ferrari and said he was in the lighting business.

I'm not entirely sure what he meant by that, but he was a true stud, and I wanted to be just like him. The more I was around this kind of lifestyle, the more intrigued and determined I became.

In contrast to the wealthy people whose carpets I cleaned, I was living in my car. After two months, I squatted in a lady's basement and did odds and ends for her. In my free time, I began working part-time for a contractor and also trying my hand

Carpet Cleanin' in California

at stand-up comedy. I had a pretty good sense of humor, and I naively figured this would ensure my success on stage. I even wrote a letter to Robin Williams after cleaning his neighbor's carpets, introducing myself and asking him to help me get started in stand-up, but he never responded.

Dead broke but determined to get out of my car and into an apartment, I worked every hour my boss could give me. Because I never turned down a job, I ended up cleaning carpets in every section of San Francisco and all the surrounding areas. This included everything from the house *Basic Instinct* was filmed in to the studio where photo shoots for *Vogue* magazine took place. I also cleaned blood and puke stains from carpets in a few rougher areas of town. If you can imagine it, I probably cleaned it, including a house where porn videos were shot.

When my boss held a contest for the tech who could sell the most cans of spot cleaner, I decided I was going to win the prize, a skiing trip to Lake Tahoe. I learned several very important things about myself in that short one-month spot cleaner contest. In fact, what I learned eventually impacted every aspect of my life.

First, I realized that I thrive on competition. I seem to have another gear in me when the pressure is on. The second thing I learned is that I'm not too shabby at sales. I like explaining the product at a level that makes sense and inspires interest. Most important, I realized that I love helping people. These three realizations became cornerstones in my life and my eventual career in life insurance.

My motivation was strong, and I ended up in a winning tie with another salesman. The beauty and sheer opulence of Lake

Tahoe made me even more determined to succeed. I wanted more of this lifestyle.

I became so good at my carpet-cleaning job that Mike, my boss, invited me to partner with him on his next franchise. This was a fantastic gesture that required serious consideration.

I told Mandy I could see myself running franchises all over the country, but who was I kidding? I was still spending my weekends at comedy clubs and open mic nights. In addition to all the writing and prep work this required, I was still taking every job I could get doing carpentry work on the side.

Aside from the fact that I was going in too many different directions at once, San Francisco was just too expensive for me. Mandy and I were always partying, always on the go, and that lifestyle took money. Mandy tried to work, but she never lasted long before getting fired for one reason or another.

One evening after we'd been drinking, Mandy and I ended up in an argument. Since we were both immature and partied too much, this was fairly common.

I left in a huff, driving too fast toward the Golden Gate Bridge, and before long I saw the inevitable red and blue lights in my rearview mirror.

After failing my sobriety test, I was arrested and taken to the San Francisco County Jail. I was there only a handful of hours, but when I got out, I had to explain the situation to Mike. In spite of my work ethic and skill, he concluded I was too much of a liability to drive his work vans.

I was devastated. With my job in shambles, Mandy and I decided to move to Ohio. We'd stay at my parents' house and get jobs and save up for our own apartment. This was a tough time, and it was no consolation to know I'd brought the situation on with my usual poor decisions.

Mandy got a job in phone sales at Ameritech while I reached out to a Chem-Dry in the city of Dayton. I didn't mention the DUI, and as far as I know, it never showed up. I was again hired on the spot, and I even found a stand-up comedy club where I was allowed to do a small five-minute set before the Sunday night comedians came on.

Before long, Mandy and I had resumed our usual routine of partying and boozing interspersed with fights about money. Predictably, she was getting homesick for California again, but at least my work was going well. When my new boss offered me a franchise in a different part of the state, it felt like déjà vu.

This time, I wasn't about to blow it by getting a DUI, but I still had to think it through. Would this job yield the degree of success I was after? Would I enjoy this work long-term? Was this what I wanted to do for the rest of my life?

The same week I was offered the franchise, Mandy and I had a fight, so I went out by myself for the evening and ran into two old friends from high school. I'd known Carl and Rich since the first grade. We'd literally grown up together, and I respected them both greatly.

Intrigued by how nicely my friends were dressed, I asked about their work and discovered they were in life insurance and making really good money. I peppered them with questions and learned that Rich ran the operations and took care of business behind the scenes while Carl focused on selling insurance and building up the agency. At the end of the evening, they offered to bring me on board.

After thinking about it for several days, I decided that selling life insurance would be more lucrative than cleaning carpets, even if I owned my own franchise. I was determined to be successful, but things were so rocky with Mandy that I had trouble concentrating. Even with Carl's assistance, I failed my licensing test the first two times I took it.

On Mandy's birthday, the day I finally passed the test, she told me she was leaving me and going back to California. She used the line "It's not you; it's me" on me, which I didn't much understand.

Later, once I'd grown up a little, I became convinced that it was in fact me. I acted like a lunatic most of the time, so I understood the dilemma she was in.

Mandy called a bunch of times after she left, but I was so mad and immature that I refused to talk to her. We'd had too many ups and downs, and I knew she wouldn't be back. Likewise, I had no intention of returning to California. My future was in Ohio, but I was so heartbroken I had a hard time focusing on my new career. It was hard to think of anything except Mandy and where we'd gone wrong.

At the same time, Mandy's leaving made me even more determined to succeed. All our fights about money and never having enough to pay our bills definitely fueled my desire to prove myself.

I was miserable, but eventually I shook myself off and began to focus on my new life in insurance along with a life without Mandy. In part, I was able to do this because of all the help I received from some very crucial people who became my friends and mentors.

EIGHT

FINDING MY SHORTCUT TO SUCCESS

> *Getting a mentor is the shortcut to success.*
>
> —BO SANCHEZ

I'm a firm believer in mentors. They can model positive attitudes, teach specific skills, offer critical insight, and help in every conceivable area of life, but I have a slightly unusual take on how to go about utilizing them.

You see, I've never once asked anyone to mentor me. I decide who my mentors are, but only I know. This is a little complicated, so stay with me.

Obviously, my mentors are people I hold in high esteem, but I decide what the lessons are. Nothing is forced because the agreement is one I make with myself and no one else.

This method allows me to learn and listen in the most natural form without putting any pressure on the mentor.

You see, I believe that when you ask people to mentor you, you rob yourself of the ability to be mentored in its purest state. The mentor is now under pressure, and helping you becomes a performance, which stifles the strongest opportunities for imitation and growth.

Maybe this is why people often say you can't learn the basics of life in school. By definition, if you're in school, you're immature. Understanding what a mentor can do for you requires maturity and humility.

That's not to say that everything the mentor says and does is always accurate, helpful, or worth emulating. You get to decide this, too, but if you're paying attention and truly want to learn, it's obvious what to imitate and what to reject.

Mentors are everywhere. You've just got to look, listen, and learn. You also have to set aside your ego so that you can ask appropriate questions and mimic or duplicate what the mentor does.

My first experience with choosing a mentor came in the navy. Little did he know, but my bunkmate Sid ended up mentoring me through every bit of ship life. He'd already been in the navy for two years by the time I showed up, so he knew the ropes. He was also up there in rank, so he was a really good guy to know and the perfect person to answer all my questions.

I also viewed the lieutenant of the division as a mentor. This was the tall, thin, stoic guy who stood so upright he was almost robotic. I only saw him when I was in trouble, but I got in so much trouble it must have seemed I was trying to sabotage myself.

Whenever my lieutenant talked to me, he tried to help me make sense of my life, but I was convinced that joining the navy had been a huge mistake. No one was going to persuade me otherwise, but he tried. I will never forget sitting on some cargo with him on one of the ship's elevators after receiving my discharge. To this day, I admire him for his willingness to talk to me when I was at my worst, and I still aspire to be like him. He set the standard for me in all my endeavors.

I met my next mentor at Chem-Dry out in San Francisco. Although Mike hired me on the spot, he did mention looking at my discharge papers. I was so afraid of losing the job that I showed up in tip-top shape, ready to work, and he never mentioned the papers again.

Mike was a great businessperson. He taught me how to talk confidently to people in their homes, he pulled out all the stops to make his clients happy, and he wasn't afraid to call a spade a spade. I didn't want to let him down, and that helped me be successful.

As always, I learned a lot because I asked a lot of questions. I developed so much respect for Mike and became so engaged in his business that I wanted to help him reach his goals. As I came to understand Mike's business model, I realized he was losing money in some areas and missing out on money in others, observations that paid off later when I had my own business.

I also learned a lot about sales from Mike. Remember the contest to see who could sell the most cans of stain remover? I really wanted to win the trip to Lake Tahoe, so I watched Mike closely during my training period. Sure enough, every person he spoke to bought the cleaner from him. I remember thinking, "This is going to be a cake walk!" Since the contest didn't start for another month, I had plenty of time to prepare.

To my surprise, once I was out on my own, I had a devil of a time convincing anyone to buy the cleaner. I couldn't understand how Mike sold it every time he cleaned a carpet. I asked whether we could ride together one day, and I even bought lunch just to get a chance to see him in action again.

Out in the field, I paid close attention to Mike's verbiage and body language. His presentation was flawless, with little apparent effort on his part. Nothing seemed obvious, but every last person purchased a can of the spot cleaner.

I told him he had to teach me how to sell this stuff, and he said, "Justin, do you have this spot cleaner at your apartment?"

"Well, no," I said. "I haven't had Chem-Dry clean it yet."

He replied, "Owners are closers."

I didn't know what that meant, so Mike explained that to own a product meant to understand it. He encouraged me to buy the cleaner so I could own it and understand it.

I said, "What's there to understand? Like you explained in the beginning, it works best on the carpets we clean."

"No, no, no," he said. "Let's go over this again."

Mike talked about the type of stain, the pH balance of the product, and the molecular level of cleaning until I realized his detailed understanding was the key to his success. Thus began my mission to learn the product and the carpet-cleaning process inside and out.

Soon, I understood the product's benefits so well that people couldn't say no. I began selling three and four cans of stain cleaner per house, all while learning the subtleties of what did and didn't work in the sales process. Soon I was neck and neck for sales with another carpet cleaner who had worked for Mike for eight years. As mentioned earlier, when the competition ended in a tie, we both got to go to Lake Tahoe.

Eventually, Mike let me start running teams of my own, and I broke records in every area of the business. He then began teaching me about franchising and the business duplication process until I understood his business model inside and out. He was a fine mentor and worked closely with me, but I've even been mentored by someone I never met.

In the early days of running my own insurance agency, when I wasn't seeing success fast enough, I decided to look into buying rental houses. This seemed like a good way to make money, but I didn't know much about it. I listened to an audiotape on the subject, and one day I saw a "for sale by owner" sign in the window of a little green house.

I followed the instructions in the audiotape regarding what to say when calling the owner and what to cover when we had our first meeting, including how much to offer, when to make the offer, and so on.

Before I knew it, I was the proud owner of my first single-family rental property, which later became twenty-one single-family rental properties. I was successfully mentored by these tapes, but that's just the beginning.

Shortly after purchasing this first property, I came across an older gentleman in the alley behind the house. He asked whether I was the new owner, and I proudly told him I was. We began to chat, and he explained that he'd been a landlord in the area for years. I knew this was someone I would want to talk to again, so we exchanged contact information.

I reached out to Darrell when I had my first issue at my rental, a problem with the water heater in the basement. My knowledge of such things was very limited, but Darrell was an expert. He showed me a few tricks of the trade, and I soaked up the information.

You see, I'm proud to be someone who readily admits what he doesn't know or understand. I can't stress the importance of this quality if you want to be successful in life. It isn't always easy to be humble, but my theory is that if you go around acting like you know everything, you'll never learn anything.

As Darrell walked me through the process of fixing the water heater, I peppered him with questions. I intended to buy more than one rental property, so I hung on every word.

Over time, based on my relentless desire to learn from him, Darrell and I became great friends. I sometimes feared I was getting on his nerves, but I can't count the times he came to my rescue when I was in a tight spot. He went out of his way to help me whenever he could.

Darrell was a true mentor and still is today, but I never asked him, "Will you mentor me?" The process was more natural than that. I had no desire to formalize our relationship, in part because I never wanted to put that kind of pressure on him. To this day, I consider Darrell a big part of my success. I turn to him for guidance, inspiration, and sometimes just an ear, and I still can't believe he took a complete stranger under his wing and taught him the ropes on how to fix up properties to rent.

Regardless of your chosen field, if you want to be successful, you have to find people like this. Even the president of the United States leans on advisors. Just be willing to give back. Offer to take those who help you out to lunch or dinner or simply lend them a hand. I spent countless hours helping Darrell improve his rental properties, all while gaining priceless insight. You simply can't put a price tag on the knowledge and friendship I gained.

As you can imagine, this method of being mentored has been an enormous factor in my success in the insurance business. It all started with my friend Carl, who along with our classmate Rich inspired me to join Lincoln Heritage and who helped me pass my licensing test. My role, like Carl's, was to sell insurance and build up the agency. This meant spending long hours recruiting and training new salespeople.

At the time I came on board, Mandy had just left me, and I was worried about paying the rent on our apartment without any help. As miserable as I was, shadowing Carl was a good distraction. I viewed him as a mentor from the very beginning. Throughout my training period, I watched every move he made, put every word he said into context, and broke his presentation down until everything he said and did made sense.

Watching him make three or four hundred dollars off a single sale was unbearably exciting. I admit that I didn't appreciate the value of insurance back then like I do now. My focus was on selling, selling, and more selling.

Become Something

After each appointment, as soon as we were back in the car, I fired questions at him. Why had he said this? Why had he waited to say that? He sometimes had to tell me to calm down because I was overthinking things, but he willingly broke each appointment down into understandable pieces that I could comprehend individually and then as a whole.

Our office was a closet-sized room in an office building. We were short on furniture, so we went dumpster-diving and found a broken desk made of particleboard. After we pieced that baby back together, Carl stuck a mirror on the inside of the desk and told me, "Every time you start to dial, open this little door, look in the mirror, and smile."

This was corny, but there was a method to the madness. It was like Carl was transferring the feeling of his smile through the phone. Once I started copying his technique, my success ratio began to soar.

Since company headquarters wouldn't give us any leads until we'd proven ourselves, our approach consisted of calling people we found in the phone book. Whenever someone was willing to listen, we explained the high costs of a funeral and offered to present a plan that would keep them from being a burden on their loved ones, or something to that effect.

Mondays, Carl and I worked from 7:00 a.m. to 9:00 p.m. trying to set up appointments for the week. It took all day and many, many calls to book the week. Being told no was the norm, but I had a good understanding of what an agent could potentially earn, so my enthusiasm seldom waned.

Eventually, we started booking appointments in Cleveland, four hours away. This meant spending a lot of time together in a car, and Carl soon tired of hearing me sing the blues about Mandy and my barren dating life. Thanks to my friend and mentor, my professional life was on the upswing, and now my personal life, too, was about to change for the better.

NINE

Stability, Turmoil, and Learning to Manage the Bit

> *It took me ten years to become an overnight success.*
> —Anonymous

First, the stability.

One day while we were driving around in between appointments with clients, Carl said, "I was at a bar the other night and ran into Jenny Price from high school; remember her?"

The name sounded familiar, so I said, "Yeah, I think so."

"I want to set you two up on a blind date," Carl continued. "Here's her number. Call her."

I thought about it for a few days and then picked up the phone. After introducing myself, I asked Jenny to go out to dinner that evening.

Become Something

When I pulled into her driveway a few hours later and caught my first glimpse of Jenny Price, blonde and beautiful, I knew immediately who she was.

In high school, a lot of girls wouldn't date me because I was always in trouble. Back then, a girl like Jenny wouldn't have come near a guy like me, so I felt a little nervous as I walked to her door.

When she opened it, her smile was so amazing that I could tell she didn't have an unfavorable view of me. A nurse at the local nursing home in the small town of Greenville, Jenny was bubbly and smart. We talked about her schooling and communicated really well, but I was still nervous. I asked her whether she liked wine and she said she did, but when the waiter came, I asked for two waters.

After a successful first date, Jenny and I began seeing each other on a regular basis. We were friends at first, but as time went by, we started to fall in love. We were rollerblading together one crisp morning when she said, "I think I'm falling for you."

This was a really cool moment that I will never forget. I might not have been brave enough to say it first, but I felt that way, too. I was also smart enough to realize I'd met the right girl at the right time, but little did I know how instrumental Jenny would be in helping me develop into the man I would eventually become.

Ironically, just as my personal life was finally straightening out, my professional life entered a sustained period of turmoil. I continued to mimic Carl's every move, but he couldn't prepare me for everything that happened out in the field. We didn't have cell phones like we do today, so getting his help meant using the client's phone and asking questions with the client listening. I truly believe clients appreciated this because they knew I wanted to do the right thing for them, but eventually my pride took over and I stopped making those calls.

Given how hard it was for me to get on top of my prospects' problems and concerns, this was a big mistake. A lot of people had similar questions about how much coverage was enough, whether they could find it cheaper elsewhere, and so on, but the nuances were always unique, and I wasn't adept at addressing them. Meanwhile, in spite of how much time I spent on the phone, I wasn't yet getting any local leads, nor was I meeting the goal I'd set of a sale per day.

The company sent out a newsletter every month identifying the state's top producers and managers. Seeing those names told me a sale a day was possible, so I decided to pick a name on that list each month. Come hell or high water, I wanted to beat that name in production the following month.

The problem was I couldn't quite do it. Every month I was a few thousand dollars off, which was nowhere close to my competition or to qualifying for the annual trip to Costa Rica the company sponsored. I really wanted to win that trip for Jenny and me, so I became obsessed with the intricacies of selling life insurance policies to complete strangers to cover their funeral costs.

Since Jenny worked the night shift, we didn't get to see each other as much as we wanted, but she was endlessly supportive. She listened to me talk about the various problems I was having and then helped me figure out ways to address them so I could meet my goals.

Become Something

Over time, with deep reflection and Jenny's input, my technique began to develop. After every appointment, I analyzed my presentation. If it hadn't ended in a sale, I wanted to know why. Sometimes I spent entire evenings pondering why I hadn't made a sale and experimenting with what I could do differently to be more successful.

Jenny's encouragement and poise throughout this process were simply amazing. I was a mediocre salesman at best, but she worked tirelessly to help me improve. It's not an exaggeration to say that her intelligence, input, and feedback were the driving force behind my success.

Meanwhile, in addition to learning how to sell life insurance policies to my own clients, I was responsible for recruiting people to the business and training them to sell. Since this was something I was compensated for, a lot of my attention was focused there.

It's a bit odd to look back at those early days when I was training people to do something I didn't fully understand myself. Perhaps that's why I felt so driven. As I analyzed the subtleties of each presentation I made, I began seeing patterns in the rejections and rebuttals. I started identifying points that needed to be made earlier rather than later, and I began asking questions and offering information to counter objections I'd received elsewhere. My ultimate goal was twofold: first, to reach the top as an individual producer and, second, to put together an effective battle-tested system that could be duplicated by those I recruited.

Unfortunately, at this stage of the game, I kept recruiting people who didn't fully understand the point of what we were doing. For example, while shadowing me, one man felt it was his duty to

Stability, Turmoil, and Learning to Manage the Bit

correct the customer on a view she held. I smoothed things over and sold that lady a policy, but on our way out, the man made a snide remark that rekindled her anger.

As we got in the car to leave, I said, "You know what you just did in there?"

He said, "I didn't do anything but help you make a sale."

He was completely clueless, but we attracted many like him in the early days. I decided to take this guy back to the office and bid him farewell, and when we arrived, I was surprised to see two police cruisers sitting in the parking lot. After our departure, the customer had become so angry that she'd called the police. I told my new recruit to wait in my office while I explained the situation.

After the police told me the customer had canceled the policy and warned me not to contact her again, I went inside. To my surprise, I found Carl packing his belongings with the new recruit sitting there watching.

"I'm outa here, man!" Carl yelled when he saw me. "Rich is a jerk, and I'm not working for him any longer. I'm going to another insurance agency, and you should come with me."

I was shocked, to say the least. I knew bad blood lingered between Carl and Rich over something that had happened years earlier, but it had never been a problem at work.

"What are you talking about?" I asked. "You can't quit. Whatever you and Rich are dealing with will blow over."

The recruit spoke up. Clueless as always, he told Carl that he'd be an idiot to leave. He got up in Carl's face several times and began taunting him. Finally, he insulted Carl with a racial epithet that mocked his Hispanic heritage.

Become Something

A moment later, wearing a ring the size of Miami, Carl hit the recruit with a right uppercut that split the guy's chin wide open and threw his head up and back. After finishing him off with a left hook and then a right, Carl growled, "He touched me first," gathered his things, and left.

The recruit was spitting blood like he was dying, so I called 911 and helped him hold his face together until the ambulance arrived. As miserable as he was, I was at least as forlorn. I had to have this job, and I was just starting to get good at it. Losing Carl was devastating, but I pressed on.

Somehow, amid all the chaos, I began putting together a very simple and effective presentation. Each time I taught it to someone, I picked up on things I was forgetting to do or needed to improve on. I was still developing a system that could be duplicated, but I was becoming a top producer simply by reflecting, seeing the holes in my game, and coming up with new answers or a better approach. However, this didn't mean my troubles were over.

Although I was recruiting new agents by running newspaper ads, I didn't have a budget from the home office to cover this expense. I had to pay for these ads out of my own pocket. I was training people at a pretty steady pace, but no one was staying long.

I was so busy that Jenny and I barely saw each other, but I ended up winning the trip to Costa Rica and qualifying as a manager and a producer. Soon I was making $400–$500 dollars a week, but only by working grueling 80-hour weeks.

On this hard-won trip to Costa Rica with Jenny, I got to meet a lot of the people I was competing with back home across the state

Stability, Turmoil, and Learning to Manage the Bit

of Ohio. It was surreal to see them in person after studying their names week in and week out.

At the bar one evening, I happened to sit next to Paul Johnson, our regional director. To me, this was like sitting next to royalty. We talked about all kinds of things, and I asked as many questions as I could get away with. I was rocked to my core when he told me he was thirty-six years old and making more than 100K a month.

I was absolutely in awe and just as intrigued. How could he be making that kind of money? He was just a normal guy with a great personality and a Southern accent that made you focus on what he was saying.

Fascinated by his evident love of what he did, I didn't leave Paul Johnson alone the entire trip. After lots of questions and one heck of a vacation, I decided I wanted to do exactly what he did. By the age of thirty-six, I too wanted to be making 100K a month.

Since I made $27,000 in the insurance business my first year after taxes, this was a lofty goal, but I made a personal commitment to reach out to Paul as often as I could without being annoying. I wanted to follow in his footsteps and mimic him to the proverbial T.

Paul must have enjoyed talking to me, too, because he actually started calling me. The best part was I held him in such high esteem and trusted him so completely that following his advice was almost easy.

You have to trust certain people in life, with the key words being "certain people." The benefits of doing so completely outweigh any rejection, betrayal, or heartbreak that might occur when you take such a chance.

Fortunately, my newest mentor was great at asking questions that forced me to see my own weaknesses, and this is how I finally learned to manage the bit. In one telling exchange, I was talking to Paul about my frustrations with a new recruit when I said something to the effect of "Forget it. This gal isn't getting it. I trained her, but a couple of months in, she's added this detail and forgotten that explanation. Her presentation is now a complete mess."

He said, "So you think she's just not going to work out?"

"I'm afraid not," I replied.

Paul asked another question or two, listened to my response, and finally said, "So most of this is on her, right?"

I laughed. "All of it's on her. She changed the presentation. She forgot stuff."

Then he asked, "Do you think you had anything to do with it?"

A big part of my pride was saying "Of course not! I know what I'm doing. I won the trip to Costa Rica, after all!"

This was the "It's not me; it's her" syndrome in action.

I shut those thoughts off and responded, "Yes, I guess I probably do."

Then he said, "Justin, *you* let the bit out of the horse's mouth."

To which I responded, "Huh?"

Paul explained that when you're training a horse, you have to patiently teach it over a consistent period of time how the bit works and which way the horse is supposed to go, including backward, forward, left, and right.

He then asked, "If I train the horse for a few days, then leave and come back in a month, how well do you think the horse will be trained?"

At that, it all clicked. I needed to spend more time with my people if I wanted them to develop fully. Instead, I typically had them ride with me for a few days and then sent them out to mimic me without taking any responsibly for my own actions or lack thereof.

I realized that I needed to truly get to know and understand the people I was hiring. I also needed to devise a more effective plan to train them. At this point in my career, I definitely wasn't a leader. I was still growing as a manager and producer even though I was finally working out the kinks in my own presentation.

Thanks to Paul, I began to understand that you can't lead a large group without genuinely appreciating that each personality is different and that the true art of management and leadership is adjusting to those personalities and understanding what makes each person tick. This also means understanding what each person is afraid of. Remember earlier in the book when I said that fear is the one thing that can stop you from achieving your dreams? In my case, fear of failure was a driver, but some people are afraid of rejection. This makes it tough to be in sales, but with self-awareness and effort, even this fear can be overcome.

Paul also helped me understand the power of a "needs and wants" analysis with new hires. Understanding the bare bones of what people need along with what they want is a powerful leveraging tool and probably one of the most important things I've ever put into practice. It's enjoyable to help people with the first part, but the real magic happens when you begin working toward the second part.

Those who are serious about meeting their goals will pick up the pace once they see in black and white that they need to work harder, faster, and smarter to get there, but other people will have developed bad habits that must be unveiled and worked through. Still others will have embraced a victim mentality and play the blame game. They won't succeed, but they'll blame everyone but themselves for their situation.

There are plenty of reasons why people don't push themselves to reach their goals, but Paul taught me to keep it simple and focus on a lack of seriousness, bad habits, or the victim mentality. Once I did this, I began to see patterns that helped me prepare for each new situation I encountered.

The most enlightening part of this process was coming to understand people at a whole new level. You really learn what makes people tick after spending time with them. The key to this is asking good questions and being a good listener, but Paul cautioned me against thinking I always had to have the answers. If you ask good questions and let people talk, he told me, they'll often figure out what the issue is and how to resolve it on their own.

He ought to know. He used this technique on me even as he taught me the more subtle intricacies of working with clients, following up on leads, and successfully spending time with my team. As I put what I learned from him into practice, I saw it begin to work like a charm.

But these were still early days. I'd made a lot of headway, but rough waters lay ahead.

TEN

PERSONAL INTEGRITY, ACCOUNTABILITY, AND GROWING PAINS

> *If you do not tell the truth about yourself, you cannot tell it about other people.*
>
> —VIRGINIA WOOLF

Personal integrity is essential to success. Unfortunately, we human beings have the uncanny ability to lie to ourselves in order to continue our bad behaviors or simply to get out of doing things we don't want to do.

Do any of these whoppers sound familiar?

"I'll quit smoking next week."

"I'll start the project tomorrow."

"I'll have the garage ready by Tuesday."

"I'll make my goal by the end of the month."

We seem to frequently fall into this vicious cycle of "I'm gonnas." A great way to avoid this is to chunk your day into realistic bites and then hold yourself accountable to whatever goals you've set.

Holding yourself accountable means refusing to lie to yourself while accepting that you are the only person who can meet your goals. Accountability partners can remind you of the goals you've set, and life coaches can give you a push when you need it, but reaching your goals is up to you and no one else.

Begin now to develop the habit of holding yourself accountable to the goals you set. This means reflecting on the tasks or goals you don't accomplish, figuring out why this is the case, and making adjustments in those areas going forward.

I have found no better tool for self-improvement than reflecting on a past situation or event to see where improvements can be made. Just be careful not to confuse looking back with dwelling on a problem. The first is good; the second is a waste of time.

For example, many comments have come my way over the years that helped shape who I am. I've been told by people I respect that I overthink things, try too hard, take things the wrong way, am too hard on myself, am negative, am hard to talk to, and plenty of other not-so-pleasant things.

None of these comments were easy to hear, but today I appreciate how meaningful and helpful such observations are when they come from people who want to help me grow.

In fact, seeking and accepting constructive criticism have become some of the most enjoyable aspects of my life. I like the challenge of improving myself based on the feedback that comes my way. I truly want to be of service to others and to improve how

Personal Integrity, Accountability, and Growing Pains

teachable I am. I also want to learn as much as I can. Nothing is more exciting to me than realizing how much better I can be if I hold myself accountable and follow through on the goals I set.

The problem is it's all too easy to be derailed. Say your goal is to find a new job that pays well. You decide to make ten contacts a day until you accept a position. You awaken Monday morning with great enthusiasm, but as the day begins, pandemonium ensues. One of your kids is sick and has to stay home with you, but you still have to take your other child to school. On your way home, you realize you have a flat tire. While you're changing it, your spouse calls to tell you she has to work late.

Before you know it, evening is at hand and you haven't reached out to a single contact. You quickly spend a few minutes blasting out résumés before going to bed, but you do it in such haste that you don't craft your cover letters properly, much less make sure you're qualified or even interested in the jobs that are available.

The rest of the week is equally chaotic, and you end up accomplishing little of substance. This is where having integrity with yourself comes into play. You are the only person who can hold yourself accountable. You made promises to yourself and let yourself down. The only way to address the problem is to devote Saturday to finding a job. This isn't how you wanted to spend the weekend, but you have personal integrity and a responsibility to meet your goals, so you do it.

I can't claim I exhibited much personal integrity or accountability in the military, but you'd better believe those traits were essential to my becoming a successful insurance salesman and manager on his way to owning his own agency. In fact, accompanied by some very memorable growing pains, personal integrity and accountability were pretty much all I had going for me early on.

You see, once I'd developed a track record, Lincoln Heritage finally began mailing me leads. This increased my potential revenue, but I was responsible for the cost of these leads and for following up on them, which meant I had to have agents to give them to. The company charged me $20–$25 a lead, and what it charged me, I charged the agents.

Like I said, I was decent at recruiting and producing; the problem was getting my people to stay long-term. Since I seldom had enough people to give the leads to, my lead balance began to grow rather large. Some time after Carl left, I expressed my concern to Rich, who basically said it takes debt to start a business.

This seemed logical, but the debt just kept growing. Before long, my balance exceeded 150K, which was a whole lot of leads not being worked. One day, Rich called to tell me a bigwig from the home office was flying out to have dinner with me and discuss something.

I had a sinking feeling this wasn't going to be good.

My production wasn't horrible, but neither was it great. At around sixty percent, my persistency, or the volume of business I was able to retain for at least a year, was a bigger issue. The biggest problem was the lead balance. It was way out of whack, and agents were continuing to leave left and right.

At dinner, our companion was dressed sharp and clearly meant business. I had developed a severe pain in my stomach earlier that day, but I wouldn't have missed this event for anything.

Personal Integrity, Accountability, and Growing Pains

I sat through the meal in excruciating pain while the boss explained that if I didn't get my persistency up, I would find myself without a job. What's more, the company had to do something about my high lead balance, so they were going to take roughly fifty percent of my pay every month until it was paid down.

I thought I was going to have a stroke on the spot, but somehow I got through the meal and walked to my car in such pain I could barely get in.

I drove straight to the hospital and learned my appendix had ruptured. After emergency surgery and a day in the hospital, I returned to work and promptly called Paul. He talked me off the ledge and helped me create a plan to tackle the issues I was up against. Together, we broke each problem into manageable parts that I could address one at a time.

Throughout this period, Carl kept calling to tell me how terrific his new company was. He constantly invited me to come check it out, so one day when I felt especially low, I visited his office.

I immediately felt like I'd walked onto the movie set of *Boiler Room*, with guys running in and out of cubicles answering phones and shuffling papers. I marveled at the pace and gazed at the unabashed reward boards positioned at the top of each cubicle. Each board was decorated with pictures of dream homes, fantasy vacation paradises, expensive sports cars, and the like. I admit it: those boards looked appealing.

Just then, Carl saw me and said, "Hey, I'm glad you're here. They're about to go over long-term care. I want you to see this;

there's a ton of money being made in that industry. It might be a great opportunity for you."

I sat down with Carl at a table in a large conference room and listened to another guy we'd gone to school with give a presentation that lasted almost an hour. It was very detailed and boring, and I knew within seconds that I wanted nothing to do with it.

As soon as I could, I explained to Carl that I appreciated the opportunity but that things were going well for me at Lincoln Heritage and I wanted to stay the course.

This wasn't exactly true, but it was certainly better than this. At least I understood the business at Lincoln and had a small team. Once again, I'd qualified for the annual trip, so even though I felt despondent, I still had reason to believe I could succeed in the end.

When I walked to my car, I saw a business card stuck in my windshield. My heart sank when I flipped it over and saw it belonged to Rich.

After chewing on this a minute, I decided to go back to the office and see whether I still had a job.

I walked in to find Rich pacing back and forth, something he did whenever he was angry.

"So what did they tell you? You going to work over there now?" he asked.

To my relief, I could see that he was worried rather than angry. I told him I was curious to see what was being offered but that I liked what I was doing and was staying put.

Rich promptly invited me to discuss our future over drinks, and later that evening we hunkered down to discuss some key changes to our business structure that would help me dig out of

Personal Integrity, Accountability, and Growing Pains

the hole I was in. We came up with all kinds of ideas for bringing on new recruits, and Rich agreed that from here on out, these new people would officially go under my umbrella. This arrangement benefitted me but also worked for Rich since he was over me contractually. Thus began the Howard Group, an agency with Lincoln Heritage Life Insurance.

Not surprisingly, I woke up the next morning with a pounding headache and an understanding that Rich and I were going to take over the world.

As I slowly began whittling away at the 150K, I often considered getting a night job, but life improved when Jenny and I began living together. She was very hardworking, and her income helped keep our heads above water.

Paul was continuing to help me see the light at the end of the tunnel, but one morning he called to say he was leaving Lincoln Heritage to start his own company. He wasn't starting an agency, he clarified. Instead, he was starting his own insurance company in partnership with his dad.

He asked whether I wanted to join him, but I couldn't do it. I had too much invested in Lincoln Heritage to walk away.

As time went by, Rich and I began to find our rhythm. We were yin and yang and climbing the proverbial ladder. He picked up where I was weak, and I believe I was strong where he was occasionally lacking. We were young, and if we kept at it, we knew we could make it to the top.

Sure enough, within three to four years, I'd met my goal of paying off the 150K. Since I'd grown accustomed to having a huge sum of money taken out of each paycheck, this was a nice shot in the arm. Better yet, I'd kept my word to my colleague, to my boss, and to myself, and things were looking up.

It isn't always easy, but if you want to live a spectacular life instead of plodding through a mundane existence, start by insisting on personal integrity. We can all make promises. We can all talk the talk. But what truly makes you follow through on your decisions is the integrity you have with yourself.

The problem is that most of us think and see outwardly. As mentioned earlier, our focus is usually on what others think. This results in self-doubt, and self-doubt is deadly. Rather than worrying about what others think or wasting time judging what they should improve on, we need to redirect that energy toward ourselves.

We see outwardly, but we cannot let that prevent us from looking inside, where true accountability lies. Not letting yourself down is essential to self-improvement. If you lie to yourself, you will end up in a vicious cycle of "Well, I'll get to it later; this is more important right now … Besides, I don't think I actually said I was going to do it anyway."

Develop the habit of setting realistic goals and meeting them. This creates true power and momentum. Simultaneously, stop worrying about what others think, do, or feel. Once you achieve the goal you've set, celebrate. Enjoy the moment and appreciate the achievement. Then get back to setting and meeting realistic goals. What's more, continually move the goal up, because it's all about making progress.

This approach will naturally keep you from developing the crippling "I bit off more than I can chew" syndrome. It's nice to dream big, but you have to set realistic goals to get there. Baby steps

Personal Integrity, Accountability, and Growing Pains

will take you all the way up Mount Everest if you keep taking them. That's why, as a practical matter, it's best to set achievable goals that will get you across the finish line.

Strange as it might sound, I believe that most people set their goals too high. When they don't achieve them, they fall into a mental funk. Consequently, they don't relax, take time off, and celebrate with the peace of mind that comes from knowing they conquered something. They never get to experience this feeling because they never achieve their goals.

Change this sad state of affairs by setting realistic goals and being honest with yourself. The more honest you are, the more achievable the process of self-improvement becomes. Not only is this approach fun but also it's where genuine self-discovery takes place.

Now—no excuses—set some realistic goals and hold yourself accountable to achieving them. Just don't be surprised when you experience a few growing pains along the way.

ELEVEN

My New Superhero

> *There is nothing either good or*
> *bad but thinking makes it so.*
> —William Shakespeare, *Hamlet*

I want to hit pause for a minute and talk about one of the most powerful abilities human beings have. I'm not trying to brag, but my brain has so much potential and strength that I can think about a dozen other things while writing this sentence.

If this claim sounds positive, think again. Our minds are capable of spectacular things, but we seldom keep them under control. That's why if I had the opportunity to be a superhero, I wouldn't choose to be Superman, Batman, or even Captain America. I'd choose to be a new superhero, one I call Concentrator.

Concentrating is something many of us do well early in life. As small children, we spend effortless hours building Lego towers,

Become Something

racing matchbox cars, or playing house with the cat, but somewhere along the way, something gives and we stop focusing like we used to.

Our minds begin entertaining far-ranging thoughts and concerns in an endless cycle, and I strongly believe our responsibilities have a lot to do with this. As adults with spouses, jobs, children, bills, and all the emotions that go along with them, it takes effort to focus on a single thought.

In my experience, those who can control their minds achieve the most in life. Likewise, those who can hone in on a task and sustain their focus seem to live most abundantly.

Today I consider myself to be a good listener, but that hasn't always been the case. As you know, I did poorly in high school. I didn't understand the power of my mind and felt no compulsion to study or excel, but something changed in the year 2000.

I was twenty-three years old and had been out of the navy for almost two years. I was living alone in a rinky-dink apartment in the middle of Ohio and had just left my job making $28,000 a year cleaning carpets in order to start selling life insurance. Mandy had just left me, and I was watching TV and wondering how in the world I was going to meet my goal of making tons of money when an infomercial came on. I heard the words "If you want to live the best life you possibly can, order my ten-day audio challenge."

The person speaking was well-known businessman and author Anthony Robbins. I certainly wanted to live the best life I possibly could, so I decided to use the last two hundred bucks I had to purchase his ten-day challenge to greatness.

My New Superhero

I was very excited when my shiny new audio collection arrived in the mail. I just knew it held the answers to all my problems and decided lack of success. It said so on the commercial, darn it!

If you're thinking, "What a sucker," hang on.

When I popped in that first CD while driving my rickety Ford Taurus down the highway, I heard, "Hi, I'm Anthony Robbins, and I'm about to rock your world" or something to that effect.

As Tony began to speak, his passion was evident. At this point in my career, I was spending a lot of time driving around from client to client. I had plenty of time to listen to Tony Robbins and soak in his ideas and enthusiasm, but a funny thing happened.

In spite of how excited I was to hear all the cool things he had to say, instead of listening intently to the recording in order to change my life, I found my mind drifting. I thought about everything *except* my brand new Anthony Robbins change-your-life audio!

Here's a sampling of what went through my mind:

"Where should I take my date for dinner tonight?"

"Man, gas prices keep going up."

"This is a filthy street; why doesn't someone clean it up?"

"Should I stop and see my parents while I'm down here?"

"I can't believe a guy just got shot on Wentworth. I was just on that street!"

"What's for lunch?"

"My phone bill's due next week."

"Look at that rickety lady crossing the street. I hope she doesn't fall."

All the while, Anthony Robbins was spitting out the goods, telling me everything I needed to know to improve my pathetic existence.

When I stopped the car to head into an appointment, it suddenly occurred to me that I couldn't remember anything I'd just heard.

This was unsettling. What was the problem?

After my appointment, I tried again. This time, I paid closer attention and realized I couldn't sustain the focus to listen to even the first hour of this ten-day series. I took a break and tried listening to the second hour, and the same thing happened again.

I struggled like this for four days.

On day five, disgusted with myself and determined to change the status quo, I started listening to the very first CD again. When I was done, I listened to it again. I'd decided I wasn't going any further until I actually understood what I was hearing.

You see, I was beginning to realize why I hadn't done well in school. I had never developed the ability to concentrate. True, I was new to the insurance business, but surely this had something to do with why I wasn't exactly killing it.

Playing that Tony Robbins audio over and over, I was amazed to realize how much information had escaped me the previous four days. For the first time in my life, I realized that getting what I wanted would require me to concentrate.

It wasn't easy, but once I was able to focus and retain the information on the first CD, a whole new world began to open up. I resumed the ten-day challenge, and it was transformational. I learned about

My New Superhero

other skills like time management and prioritizing and addressing limitations and began incorporating them into my life.

As I actively listened to these audios, I found myself frequently hitting the pause button so I could write down concepts I wanted to review later. I found Robbins's words and thoughts so simple, so exciting, and so encouraging that in addition to concentrating, I began to develop a new skill: the ability to discipline myself. I wanted to get through the ten days in part because of how awesome the CDs were but also because I didn't want to screw up something that could actually improve my life.

I stuck to the program relentlessly, and at the end of the ten days, I felt an awesome sense of accomplishment I'd never before experienced. For the first time ever, I'd pursued something and completed it. Tony taught me not only all the skills I needed to live a wonderful life but also what it was like to finish a task I'd set out to do!

I wanted more, so I began purchasing every Anthony Robbins audio I could find. My concentration and comprehension levels grew with every audio I listened to, further cementing my realization of the importance of controlling the mind.

Could it be a coincidence that my income began steadily increasing, too?

I don't think so. The information I was taking in was so inspiring and compelling that it affected my attitude and resolve. I realized that if Tony Robbins could make this audio with so much passion and conviction, I could surely get off the couch and make something of myself.

For me, success started with concentration and its logical child, comprehension. After that came discipline. These are skills some people learn early, some people learn late, and some people never learn. I was almost in that final category, and I'll always be grateful to Tony Robbins for the role he played in helping me improve myself.

People often say things like "That experience changed my life," but I don't believe that can happen until they develop the ability to truly focus, concentrate, and comprehend what it is they're experiencing. Listening to Tony Robbins truly did change my life, but only after I developed this elusive ability.

If you're like me and find it hard to concentrate, think about what might become possible if you embrace the hard work it takes to master this challenge.

I work with many people who genuinely struggle to focus, and I can proudly say I did too, once upon a time, but not anymore. From the bottom of my heart, let me convey my belief that if I can do it, you can do it. All your desires, all your dreams, really can come true if you will just hone in on this dual strategy of concentration and comprehension.

I still catch my mind wandering at times, but I have greatly improved this muscle between my ears. There's a saying that if you can do something ten thousand times, you will master it. If that's true, I'm well on my way to mastery!

Genuinely being in any given moment takes pure concentration, energy, and focus. Form these good habits and make them your masters. Developing such discipline is like any other skill you learn. Yes, it's incredibly hard at first, but so is training any other muscle in your body. The more you do it, the stronger you get. Until now, I hadn't committed to doing this, but now it was all finally coming together.

I don't make promises lightly, but I promise you this: if you will learn to be in the moment and concentrate, you will create a more abundant and prosperous life than you ever dreamed possible.

TWELVE

IT MIGHT BE YOU

> *The buck stops here.*
>
> —Harry S. Truman

Are you happy? What is your mind saying right now if you pause long enough to listen? Are your thoughts happy or sad, colorful or black, clear or confusing?

The greatest thing about the mind is that we can control our thoughts. Believe it or not, our thoughts are one of the few things we *can* control in life. We can choose what to think like and be like. We can choose to see things as awesome and fantastic, or we can choose to see things as dark and depressing. This is a simple fact.

By extension, we also hold the power to experience things the way we choose to. Think of the great disparity in how people react to something as simple as a movie. When it ends, one person walks out on cloud nine, feeling like her life has changed for the better, while the second person hates the movie so much that he walks up to the ticket booth and demands his money back. Both individuals decide what they want to see, and both find what they're looking for.

That's how life works. You decide what you're looking for, and then you go out and find it. You might disagree or say it can't be that simple, but it really is. Let's use me as an example.

Long ago, before I joined the navy, I decided I wanted to be successful in life. That was a straightforward goal; I simply wanted to be successful. In part, that's why I was so miserable in the navy. I felt like I was on hold and unable to follow through on my goal.

As you know, my first job after the military was cleaning carpets. I was a very good carpet cleaner, if I do say so myself. Along with my decision to be successful, I brought with me a few tools I knew I'd need. My toolbox wasn't very large yet, but I did bring a strong work ethic. I was determined to get the job done no matter what.

The second thing I brought with me was my personality, something I will always be grateful for. I can't stress enough how important a sense of humor is to a great and abundant life. You absolutely must know how to laugh, and if you don't, I strongly encourage you to develop this ability. If you can't laugh, and by extension if you can't laugh at yourself, you'll be miserable.

The last thing I brought was my determination to succeed. I had a white-hot fire in my belly urging me to make something of myself.

It Might Be You

With these tools, I worked very hard cleaning carpets. I was never late, I never complained, and I was always cheerful about working extra hours. In short, I had a good attitude and was game for anything that would prove I could handle the task before me.

Fast-forward to my early years in the insurance business. It's hard to admit this, but I became way too cynical and frankly not very nice to be around. I probably uttered the words "What the hell?" a hundred times a day.

At the time, I thought this was because so many new sales recruits were burning me. It makes me a bit uncomfortable to admit this, given how far I've come, but when I first started training people, I didn't pay much attention to the miles I was putting on myself.

Over time, I began to feel like everyone was trying to pull something over on me. After years of not realizing what the real problem was, I fell into a trap of cynical jadedness. I was mentally always preparing for people to try to take advantage of me.

Sooner or later, most of us go through a version of this. Some of us pick up on the root cause, but others never see what's truly going on. Those of us who get caught in this vicious cycle of self-defense sometimes find it spirals out of control to the point that we never get out of it.

For years, I was stuck in this cycle, unable to comprehend that I was causing my own frustration. I will never forget the aha moment that came one day as I was leaving a lady's house after she sternly told me she wasn't interested in a life insurance policy and slammed the door behind me.

While walking off her porch, I had the sudden and clear realization, "Wait a minute; the problem is me!"

Become Something

For the first time in my life, I took ownership of myself. I realized this lady had slammed the door on me because I'd brought my life and problems into her house. That morning, I'd encountered a number of rude individuals on the phone, had endured disappointing interactions with my salespeople, had left my ATM card in the machine ... I could go on and on, but for the first time in my life, I took responsibility for my attitude and realized my problem wasn't the leads, the company, the salespeople, the weather, the news, or my clients. I was my problem.

I talked to Jenny about this and started thinking more deeply about how I contacted clients and presented policies with the goal of meeting *their* needs, not my own.

With utter clarity, I finally accepted that the only thing I had control over was my attitude.

Once I accepted this, I also began to realize that the people around me were there as a result of a decision I'd made. *I'd* decided to hire people to work for me. No one told me I had to do it; I'd decided to do it. That also meant I'd decided whom to hire. Again, this was my decision and no one else's.

On this journey through self-awareness, I started honing in on my experience with new recruits. I'd hired and trained thousands of them, and nearly every one of them told me about all the great things they were going to do that they never followed through on. I'd not only swallowed a lot of lies about their accomplishments, capabilities, and so on, but I'd also eaten hundreds of thousands of dollars of debt believing them.

After years of dealing with this, I started to think that everyone lies, yet the solution wasn't cynicism or feeling suspicious and superior. I needed these recruits. I also needed to understand that each new person was ultimately responsible to himself or herself. Finally, I needed to take responsibility for my part in the equation.

If I failed to pay attention to the fact that a prospective employee was twenty-five minutes late to our interview and walked in wearing jeans and a T-shirt, whose fault was it? If I overlooked the fact that someone showed up for work smelling like alcohol, whose fault was it? If I just nodded when someone told me, "I'm not here to be interviewed; I'm hear to see whether I'm interested in a position," whose fault was it?

It was my responsibility to tell prospective employees they needed access to a vehicle to work for me. It was my responsibility to tell these same people they needed to be able to work weekends and couldn't be done every day at 3:00.

But I will also tell you why I used to let people walk all over me: I was desperate beyond belief to grow my business, and that desperation led me to become cynical when people didn't live up to my expectations.

Until this epiphany hit me, I blamed everything and everyone I could think of for my problems. Here's a little secret: the blame game is usually the first indication of a bad attitude.

After I came to this conclusion, everything changed for me, including the hiring process. Going forward, I stopped taking it personally when recruits let me down. More importantly, they were letting themselves down. I also promised myself I'd hire the right people from here on out instead of hiring out of desperation. This slowed things down initially, but I ended up with the right employees in the long run, which saved a lot of time, energy, and hassle.

Become Something

It's when you finally decide you're going to hire people because they're a great fit for your culture or business environment that companies grow in leaps and bounds. That like-mindedness is where the true magic takes place. It's easy to see that having multiple people on the same page allows businesses to grow and flourish. Looking at it from this perspective reveals how critical the hiring process truly is.

No matter how old you are, when you finally realize that maybe the problem is you, your whole life will change for the better. When you accept the fact that you might be taking yourself too seriously and this might have something to do with why things aren't going the way you want them to, it's like someone handed you the secret to life.

That's why I hope you'll resist the urge to be cynical. Just because one person does something hurtful or bad to you doesn't mean everyone is going to—in fact, far from it. I truly believe most people are good in their hearts and aren't out to do any harm. You just have to trust that notion instead of assuming everyone you meet is trying to take advantage of you. Those things happen, but you need to learn from those experiences without letting them turn you into a pessimist. Listen to your heart, your gut, or whatever faith you practice, and trust.

This doesn't mean everything will go your way, of course. Back when I was still single and trying to do stand-up comedy, I finally had to accept that while I've always been able to laugh at myself, I'm not actually funny. Instead, I'm just easily amused.

It Might Be You

I'm not too happy about this fact of life, but I have to accept it and have a good attitude about it. We all have limitations, but we all have the ability to be successful, too.

Truth be told, I still sometimes have to work to keep my attitude in check. I've even come up with a safeword I use to remind myself that I'm on the verge of losing my cool.

Whenever I feel like I'm about to blow a gasket, I mentally take a step back. As needed, I think or say my safeword out loud and then try to find a silver lining. This technique might sound corny, but it works for me and helps me avoid taking myself too seriously.

Next time you're frustrated with something, next time you have a bad attitude, next time you feel cynical and dismissive of people, ask yourself, "Is it me?" If you do this, your life will change for the better.

Our nature as human beings makes us want to reject the idea that we might have something to do with what's bugging us, but if we can just come to terms with the fact that we bear some responsibility for whatever situation we're dealing with, we empower ourselves, finally, to do something about it.

This is progress, and in my book, progress has a lot to do with happiness and with that innate desire to become something that has driven me all my life.

THIRTEEN

NO SUCH THING AS A PROBLEM

> *I don't see problems;*
> *I see opportunities for improvement.*
>
> —STEVE JOBS

The problem with problems isn't the problems themselves—everyone has them, and everyone deals with them differently. The problem lies in how we see our problems. I hope this chapter will help you see your problems as nothing more or less than an opportunity for improvement.

Rather than think things like "I have the worst luck" or "This always happens to me," why not copy Jack Ma, founder of Alibaba, who says that all true magical ideas are born out of complaints? He recommends looking into the complaint and solving it in order to yield the essential product or idea.

Become Something

By extension, if you want to experience success in your life—real happiness and success in every area of life—you have to start with what consumes your mental energy.

Most of us don't realize how much energy our thoughts consume, but children are good examples of how this works. I have a two-year-old and a three-year-old, and when we take them to new places, they are exhausted at the end of the day because of how much energy their brains use.

Grown-ups are no different, but once we develop a lot of skills, we think we have all the answers to life's problems. This is why we seldom approach new situations with open minds. On the contrary, most of us continuously wear ourselves out with negative and irrational thoughts that waste good energy. We all know the challenges of the day will naturally consume our energy, but what role does our attitude toward these challenges play?

A great deal, as it turns out. After reading a book that made me realize how much energy most people squander judging others and complaining, I recently embarked on the challenge of going a full twenty-four hours without doing either.

To my surprise, I found I was so accustomed to judging other people and complaining that I literally could not eliminate both habits simultaneously.

I focused on extinguishing my habit of complaining first and was quickly forced to confront several questions, at least in the privacy of my own mind. Namely, was life as riddled with problems as my attitude indicated? Did I complain as much at home as I did at work? How did Jenny stand it, and what kind of impact might this habit be having on our sons?

No Such Thing As a Problem

Consciously watching myself enter my customary negative state as the twenty-four hours began made me aware of how natural it was and also liberated me to do a 180. I deliberately began focusing on the silver lining in each situation I normally complained about. I also began enjoying the challenge of trying to see the good in every situation—and I do mean every situation, whether trivial or momentous. Whenever I felt a complaining thought or comment beginning to form, whether it involved work or something at home, I shifted my thoughts until I could find something good in the situation.

It helped to remember how, as a child, my mother always said, "Honey, everything happens for a reason." At the time, I'd just shrugged these words off, but now I began to appreciate the wisdom behind them. When you start finding the good in everything, it's almost like a higher power saying, "Hey, pay attention! I'm trying to teach you something that's going to help you and possibly even save your life!"

For instance, say I get a flat tire that strands me on the side of the road for an hour. Who's to say that flat didn't happen for a reason? Perhaps it stopped me from colliding with a drunk driver down the road who would have plowed into the side of my car and killed me.

As I stopped routinely complaining over the twenty-four-hour period, I noticed a distinct increase in my energy level. I felt happier, and the people around me seemed happier, too.

Spurred on by these obvious benefits, I embarked on phase two of the challenge. To my dismay, I found it just as hard to stop judging other people as it was to stop complaining. Nonetheless, I mindfully set myself to the task of doing this over a twenty-four-hour period.

Focusing on the fact that I didn't have all the information I needed to make a judgment and that it wasn't my place to judge others in the first place helped. As I mindfully eliminated the negative energy I customarily displayed, I again noticed my energy levels increasing along with my positive outlook.

Now, some time after this experiment, I find myself far more aware of my innate tendency to spread negativity by complaining and judging others. This awareness has helped me develop the infinitely more positive habit of looking for the good in life. We get only one shot, so why not make the best of it?

In my opinion, the only way to find true happiness and success is to first work on improving the core of who you are. This journey begins in the mind, and it requires us to pay attention to all the negative thoughts we entertain. The goal is not merely to eradicate these thoughts but to turn them around by honing in on the opportunities they hold.

For example, one harmful notion many of us start believing early in life is that if we don't know something, we'll look stupid. Just today on a conference call, I was discussing how my success in life can partly be attributed to the fact that I don't feel embarrassed when I don't know something. By contrast, I've often noticed a lack of participation or involvement in people who fear someone might realize they don't know something. All I can say is what a wasted opportunity!

To be successful, you have to realize how powerful it is to learn things you don't already know. To really learn, you have to cast

No Such Thing As a Problem

judgments and distractions aside so that you can focus on what you're learning.

To me, living fully means learning constantly, so it's peculiar to see how often people stymie their progress in this regard. I've been training people in sales and management since 2004, and I'm always amazed at how large a role the ego plays. Most folks become defensive when they don't know something and consequently miss out on a great opportunity to learn. I can't tell you how many times I've heard someone say, "Oh, I know," when in fact the person has no idea what I'm talking about.

Whenever I have the opportunity to learn something that's vital to my understanding and to living a more fulfilling life, I get super excited. More accurately, I've trained my brain to get super excited, something along the lines of, "Hurrah! I have an opportunity to improve this area of my life!"

Typically, I try to get my hands on a book on the subject. For example, if I'm having a problem understanding my two-year-old, I'll pick up a book on parenting toddlers. If I find myself in a complicated selling and commission opportunity, I'll seek out a book that details creative new sales techniques. As obvious as this approach sounds, it's actually one of the least frequently implemented tactics to living an abundant, fulfilling, happy life.

Perhaps it goes without saying, but don't forget to implement what you learn. You don't get great at playing the violin by reading about it. You don't master jujitsu by watching videos of other people on the mat. You become great by practicing these skills yourself.

Become Something

I truly believe we are put on this earth to find out who we are and how we can benefit ourselves and others now and in the future. We can always change and improve, and the process and outcome are absolutely beautiful. We can do and be anything we want in life. What others have done, we can do. We can change ourselves simply by making the decision to do so!

Another way to look at problems is to think about them from the perspective of a benefactor. Early in my insurance career, I came across a quote by Zig Ziglar that helped shape my approach to selling life insurance: "You can have everything you want in life if you will just help enough people get what they want."

At first, the selfish part of me understood only the first part—"You can have everything you want in life"—without really comprehending the second part—"if you will just help enough people get what they want."

It takes maturity and selflessness to understand and put into practice the second part, but when you do, you begin to experience the tremendous joy of helping others.

When I first started out in insurance, I had a tiny office, the broken desk Carl and I found in the dumpster, a phone book, and a license to sell life insurance. I began each morning by randomly opening the phone book and calling the numbers on whatever page I landed on. Whenever someone answered, I attempted to set an appointment to discuss planning for their funeral and final wishes.

This wasn't the easiest thing in the world to do, but I earnestly did my best. As I made these calls, I mindfully experimented with aspects of my performance. As you know, I discovered that if I smiled and incorporated a sense of humor, the calls went better.

No Such Thing As a Problem

Consequently, I began smiling into the mirror Carl put on the inside door of my desk. I had realized that my enthusiasm and positive energy played a role in the conversation to follow.

Please don't misunderstand what I mean by saying energy plays a role. I'm not advocating being loud and boisterous. What I mean is that I focused my energy on each moment and call. With experience, I came to realize it was in my best interests to match the energy level and tone of the person I was calling. If the person on the other end spoke enthusiastically, I spoke enthusiastically. If the person spoke lethargically or in a monotone, I likewise spoke in a subdued fashion.

Movement helped, too. I soon realized that if I was moving or at least standing, the calls went better. I've heard salespeople say "Motion creates emotion," and there's some truth to that. I usually gave a few karate kicks or punches in the air whenever I set an appointment, making a quick workout a nice fringe benefit of success.

I also learned that certain times of the day were better than others to make these unsolicited calls. For example, calls later in the evening netted better results than the 4:30–7:00 time frame, when I was interrupting dinner or its preparation.

The more people I reached out to and booked appointments with, the more people I had a chance of selling a life insurance policy to, so I took these insights extremely seriously. Even better was realizing I could teach these skills to others. I could better their lives and be compensated for it to boot!

This, my friends, is where the rubber hit the road. At this realization, I was in all the way, even if I didn't yet know how to smoothly accomplish these challenging tasks.

Become Something

My wife has a friend who continually takes classes to enhance her nursing skills and credentials. From a monetary perspective, she makes an increasingly comfortable living simply because she constantly has new expertise and knowledge to pass on to others.

The same goes for doctors, lawyers, and virtually every type of professional you can think of. The person with the most knowledge usually gets paid the most. That's why you can literally start from nothing and become something—and not only become something but also become everything you want to be!

Let me emphasize that you can start anywhere and achieve greatness. I don't need to provide a long list of all the greats who started with nothing, but I want to give a couple of examples.

Take Richard Branson, founder of Virgin Records. He literally started from nothing when he founded a magazine on campus at his school. Jeff Bezos, the founder of Amazon, started selling books online out of his garage. Steve Jobs and Steve Wozniak, founders of Apple, likewise started building and selling computers out of a garage. William Harley started out in a small shed trying to build an engine for a bicycle; he later started the motorcycle giant we all know as Harley-Davidson.

What did these people have in common? They saw problems as opportunities and began to do things better, smarter, faster, and easier simply by *doing*. They were able to benefit other human beings by continuing to gain knowledge along the way.

Remember: there's no such thing as a problem. Instead, there are infinite opportunities to develop the attitude that allows us to use our energy to improve life for ourselves and those around us.

FOURTEEN

READY TO COMMIT?

> *There is always room at the top.*
>
> —DANIEL WEBSTER, ATTRIBUTED

Most people are interested in improving their lives. The problem is they're not *committed* to improving them. Without commitment, nothing really lasts, whether it's a marriage, a skill, or a career.

When I think about the success I've achieved and the success I hope to help you achieve, I can't help but conclude that commitment involves setting goals and making plans that enable success. Some of this preparation is lofty and some is downright mundane, but it's all an essential part of the setup. Without this setup, success is elusive.

Become Something

For example, when I first jumped into selling life insurance, one thing immediately became obvious: I'd better learn how to read a map. Sound silly? These were the days before GPS on a cell phone told you what turn to take. If you couldn't read a map, you couldn't reach your destination. Simply put, I realized I wouldn't be able to reach my destination unless I knew how to get there.

This statement is so important that I want to repeat it. *I realized I wouldn't be able to reach my destination unless I knew how to get there.*

Isn't that how life works? If you want to be successful in life, you have to have a plan. You have to prepare. You have to have goals. And then you have to commit to meeting them. Just like I couldn't reach my destination without a map, I couldn't reach success without planning for it and committing to it.

I'm a big believer in this process. I know it works because I've proven it over and over. Frankly, there's nothing more exciting to me than visualizing a tangible goal, creating a doable plan, and then following through to bring it to fruition.

Many people forget that they will encounter obstacles during this process. Just remember that problems are merely opportunities in disguise. It takes patience, time, and tenacity to overcome these hurdles, but I find it exciting to have some mystery involved in what lies ahead. That's actually something I love about the process.

A lot of people talk about "passion." They say you have to be passionate about your product or service to be successful. I agree, but something is missing from this advice, and that's having passion about the process of building a great *you*.

Successful people embrace the fact that they're developing. Want to be one of them? Commit to reading a book per month on a given subject and mindfully putting into practice the things you learn. Commit to starting that business you've thought about for the past decade. Commit to finding that mentor to help you troubleshoot the problems you have at work. Commit to taking that class to develop the skills you need to pursue the career you truly want.

Once again, Zig Ziglar said it best: "You can be a meaningful specific or a wandering generality."

Don't settle for being a wandering generality! Instead, imagine life as you want it to be. Use your imagination and take the time to figure out what a great life looks like for you. Think money and finances, love and relationships, possessions and desires, service and satisfaction—anything you can think of that will help you design the life of your dreams. Again, think outside the box and *dream*.

If you need a little inspiration, take a moment to visit your local bookstore and leaf through the luxury lifestyle magazine called the *Robb Report*. This magazine helped me realize that the world contained opportunities I'd never dreamed of as an eighteen-year-old enlistee in the navy. In so doing, it helped me to dream much bigger dreams than I had in the past.

Once you've taken the time to think about what a perfect life looks like for you, start putting your plan in place. Let's say you work as a cashier at a restaurant and want to become a manager. It's absolutely amazing what can happen if you'll just take the time to come up with a plan.

Not surprisingly, the position of manager pays better than cashier but requires more skills. To position yourself for this career, you need to know exactly what responsibilities it entails and be fully committed to achieving this goal. (Note: the half dozen fast-food chains I've worked at in my life didn't make me a millionaire, but you'd better believe they helped me become one because all the time I worked for them, I was gaining skills and dreaming big.)

Once you've established what you need to do to reach the level of management, put the ball in motion. Develop the missing skills, fill out the application, prepare for the interview, dress for success, and so on.

Perhaps you have small children and need to figure out who will watch them while you're at work. Perhaps you're in school and need to get creative about accommodating both your academic and work schedules. Perhaps someone else beats you to the punch and is awarded the position you're after. Or perhaps your plan is delayed until the position becomes available.

So what? Use your newfound skills of personal integrity and accountability to stick to your goal no matter what comes along to derail you. You don't actually need anything to be successful but a hunger for a better life and a commitment to follow through on the goal you've set.

That said, planning is definitely the sticking point for most people. Either they don't take the need to plan seriously or they conclude they can't make it all work. Successful planning requires asking tough questions, and it usually requires making sacrifices, too.

Understand that the goal is number one. The goal is everything. It's a declaration, a pledge, and an obligation, so don't lie to yourself. Make the commitment. Accept the challenges and constraints of your life and begin planning how to reach your goal in spite of them. You can do this; it simply requires concentration and will. If your problem is childcare, figure it out. If it's your spouse's schedule, figure it out. I could keep going, but you get the picture.

Of course it's tough. Anything worth doing is tough. Art Williams, one of my favorite speakers, asks people to tell him their problems and then invariably comes back with a simple response:

Person: Well, Art, you see I always wanted to [fill in the blank].
Art: Well, then, just do it!
Person: Yeah, but Art, I want to become somebody.
Art: Okay, then, do it!
Person: I want to be financially independent.
Art: Then do it!

If you want to live the life of your dreams, do it! If you want to sing that song, if you want to write that book, if you want to start that company, if you want to become a public speaker, if you want to meet that company goal, if you want to pay off that debt, if you want to lift those weights, if you want to create a better life than the one you currently have, do it!

It really is that simple, so take the time to figure out what's holding you back. Once you do this, you can fill out the paperwork, prepare for the interview, do your meal planning and shopping in advance, and so on. Then, when the fur hits the fan, you'll be prepared. You'll make yourself one hundred percent capable of reaching

Become Something

your goal, whatever it happens to be, because you've committed to doing so.

Throughout this process of committing to your goal, be careful to show up with your best every single day. This means wearing a smile and staying positive no matter what. It means never complaining.

Remember my recent goal to go twenty-four hours without complaining or judging others? It wasn't easy, but this important exercise helped me become aware of how often I'm unpleasant to be around, both at the office and at home. Getting on top of this has made life a lot more pleasant, and I feel good knowing I'm doing the right thing and taking personal responsibility for something that impacts everyone around me.

Try this challenge yourself. If you're a complainer like me, maybe you'll want to start with challenging yourself to go twenty-four hours without complaining. Developing this counter-skill—the inability to complain—is an essential element of self-improvement. I promise you right here and now that someone has it worse than you do. Somewhere, probably not too far away, someone is in a *way* worse position than you are. Sorry to be so dramatic, but that's the fact.

People always look up to noncomplainers, people always ask for help from noncomplainers, people always respect noncomplainers. No matter what their circumstances, noncomplainers stand out as a beacon of hope. Displaying this quality in the workplace will absolutely help you achieve your goals. When you eradicate complaining from your behavior, not only will you be far more likeable and leader-like but also you will naturally go into solution mode.

Along the same lines, do not under any circumstances get involved in gossip. Remember playing the game called Telephone as a kid? Remember how garbled the message became by the time it reached the end of the line?

Gossip in the workplace works pretty much the same way, but unlike the game of Telephone, it takes an emotional toll. I remember reading about a concept called transference of feelings early in my career. It basically means you redirect the feelings you have for one person to another person. In the case of gossip, which is inherently negative, transference of feelings can adversely affect how you feel about others—fairly or unfairly—as well as how you feel inside.

Instead of letting gossip inform my opinions, instead of speaking negatively about those who aren't there to defend themselves, I prefer to assess people based on the personal interactions we have. This practice has served me very well socially and at work. It helps me show up with my best, and when you show up with your best every day, you become very attractive.

When you are very attractive, clients, owners, and employees will want to see more of you, and you will be recognized for your talents, skills, and abilities with appropriate promotions and compensation. This is the natural trajectory, and it all starts with committing to the process of setting goals, planning for success, and being the best you can be.

Just remember that without such a commitment, nothing really lasts. In this case, nothing begets nothing. How could it be otherwise?

CONCLUSION:

GET YOURSELF A REASON WHY

> *I have a dream.*
>
> —MARTIN LUTHER KING JR.

Virtually everything we use, touch, and see exists because someone was committed to a dream.

Another way of saying this is that this person was committed to his or her *why*.

If you have a big enough reason why, you'll do whatever it takes to achieve what you want in life. I don't mean to insult anyone, but if your reason isn't big enough, your excuses probably are.

Maybe your why is that you have something to prove.

Maybe your why is that you want to create a wonderful life for someone, including yourself.

Become Something

Maybe your why involves your children—perhaps you want them to have more opportunities than you did growing up.

Maybe your why is borne out of a gut instinct or belief in what your heart or mind is telling you to do.

Maybe, like Dr. Martin Luther King, you feel driven by your desire to annihilate racism.

Maybe you want to help people learn a specific skill.

Whatever your reason, your why is the answer. If it's strong enough, it will catapult you into the life of your dreams and keep you concentrating and focused throughout the toughest times you face. It will be a constant reminder and a directional beacon, always there to support you no matter the odds or circumstances.

In 1919, Walt Disney was fired from the *Kansas City Star* because he "lacked imagination and had no good ideas."

Good thing his why wasn't listening.

When the Beatles auditioned for Decca Records in 1962, Dick Rowe told their manager, Brian Epstein, "Guitar groups are on their way out."

Good thing their why didn't care.

There is nothing stronger in this world than people who are truly committed to their why, so hone in on yours. It will be challenged many times in life, but you have to have the strength to pursue it anyway.

If you're not sure what your why is, let me help you find it. Take emotion out of the equation for a moment and think about what you truly want in life. Once your canvas is blank, start throwing paint at it like da Vinci on steroids.

Conclusion: Get Yourself a Reason Why

Ask yourself, "If I could have anything I want at this very minute, if there were no limitations whatsoever, what would it be?"

Again, ask yourself, "What do I want?"

This time, put the emphasis on the final word: "What do I *want*?"

Once you know what you want most of all, answer this question: "Why?"

There it is. That's it. It really is that simple! Whether you like it or not, this is the catalyst that will get you moving and grooving.

You're probably thinking, "It can't be that simple," but I assure you it is. Your why is the key, the password, the entry point, to all the potential you possess. It will direct you to the abilities, skills, and wisdom you hold inside that you might not even know exist. Your why holds the truth about who you are, but don't let that scare you. Instead, let it shed light on your true abilities and potential.

Understand your why for what it is: the reason you get up and move, the reason you study, the reason you stay awake at night, and the reason you sometimes feel angry. That's how powerful your why is. It controls your emotions subconsciously.

You have only one chance to make the most of life, so if you truly want to experience fulfillment beyond belief, discover your why. After you discover it, listen to it, learn from it, chase it, and above all trust it to guide you to what you're looking for. You've heard the phrase "Trust your instincts"; your instincts are your why knocking at the door. Trust your why. Open the door.

I have many whys, and one involves my mom. When I was a young boy, I overheard her tell her friend that Elvis Presley had just bought his mother a pink Cadillac for her birthday. I remember my mother saying how neat it was that a son would buy his mother a brand-new car.

I took that to heart and decided right then and there to buy my mom a pink Cadillac someday. Why? I wanted to make my mother extremely happy. It was as simple as that! I would tell her periodically through life, "I'm going to get you that pink Cadillac one day, Mom."

To her, it was the thought that counted, but I was determined to follow through on this promise. My why burned inside me. Today, I can proudly say that I've bought my mom not only a red BMW (Mary Kay ruined it for the pink Cadillac) but also a blue one. I will continue to buy my mom a new car every year because I love to see her happy. What a powerful why!

By now, I hope it's apparent that my why also drives my desire for self-improvement and my relentless efforts to get better, smarter, sharper, and evermore positive. When you can maintain optimism regardless of what you're dealing with, you're better able to deal with the situation at hand while preparing yourself for future challenges.

It's probably not possible to stay happy-go-lucky all the time—this is something I definitely struggle with—but I do know that if you can maintain a positive self-regard and an optimistic perspective, you will live an extraordinary life.

How do I know this? Because personal development and success *always* go together. Once I learned to master my emotions, I began to thrive, and that's when I put myself in a position to become something.

Even during those times when I felt my lowest, such as when Uriah died, when I was in the navy, when Mandy left me, and when I was deeply in debt to Lincoln Heritage, I had this crazy

Conclusion: Get Yourself a Reason Why

sense that I was in that particular place and time for a reason. I always knew deep in my heart that I was someone special. I always wanted to make my parents proud and happy, and I always wanted to repay them for taking such good care of my brother and me.

Now that you know how I turned my life around and used my why to become something, it's your turn. What is your why? What makes you tick day in and day out? What makes you do what you do?

Now ask yourself a serious question. Does your why need an evaluation or adjustment? In other words, have you lost sight of your why and become complacent and stagnant?

This happens to a lot of people, but I hope you won't let it happen to you. If it is happening, how long do you intend to let it go on? A day? A month? A year? A lifetime?

Some people make the mistake of living their entire lives in complacency, while others stay there a short time and move on. Recognizing that you've possibly become complacent offers a fantastic opportunity to reevaluate your why. Sometimes we just need to spring-clean our thoughts, but be careful not to start worrying about what other people think.

It bears repeating that whatever you hold in the highest esteem, whatever makes you happy, is no one else's business. If you let other people's thoughts and opinions affect you, you'll dismantle the whole process of finding your why and therefore your way. That's a shame, because what a wonderful process it is once you say to yourself, "My why is for me and only for me, and nothing is going to get in the way."

Become Something

Tell yourself, "There are no distractions from my why" and "I cannot let anything in life stand between my why and me."

Let your why drive why you go to work, why you eat, why you live. That's how powerful it is, so commit to it. Let it create the abundant life you so fervently desire.

Once you do, you'll become something, all right—the person you were truly meant to be.

About the Author

Justin Howard was born in Tampa, Florida, in 1975 and moved with his family to rural Ohio when he was three. Upon graduating from Greenville High School in 1995, he joined the navy. Two years later, he moved to California, where he worked as a carpet cleaner. Shortly after returning to Ohio, he began selling life insurance. He started building teams in 2000, and by 2005, he was life coaching. The owner and CEO of the Howard Group, an agency with Lincoln Heritage Life Insurance Company, he now employs three hundrend people. Married to his beloved wife Jenny, with whom he has two small sons, he lives with his family in Dayton, Ohio.